THE ESSENTIAL GUIDE TO
Professional Horse Care

THE ESSENTIAL GUIDE TO
Professional
Horse Care

ALISON
POCKLINGTON

J. A. ALLEN

© Alison Pocklington 2004
First published in Great Britain 2004
ISBN 0 85131 868 1

J.A. Allen
Clerkenwell House
Clerkenwell Green
London EC1R 0HT

J.A. Allen is an imprint of Robert Hale Limited

A catalogue record for this book is available from the British Library

Design by Judy Linard
Colour separation by Tenon & Polert Colour Scanning Limited, Hong Kong
Printed by Midas Printing International Limited, China

Contents

Acknowledgements   vi

Introduction   vii

1   Horse Health   1
2   Care of the Foot and Shoeing   19
3   Grooming and Turnout   26
4   Clipping   55
5   Feeding   66
6   Fittening   111
7   Tack and Equipment   130
8   Travelling   175
9   Competition Preparation   203
10 Care of the Horse at a Competition   213
11 Care of the Horse at a Three-Day Event   234
12 Roughing Off   269

Epilogue   276

Index   277

Acknowledgements

The line drawings in this book are all by Maggie Raynor. All photographs in this book are by Matthew Roberts with the exception of those on pages 224, 226, 227, 238, 257 (bottom), 258 which are by the author and that on page 218 which is by Nick Morris.

The author and publishers are grateful to Kenilworth Press for permission to base the diagram 'Condition Scoring' on page 93 and to use the accompanying text from that used in *The BHS Complete Manual of Stable Management* which was published by Kenilworth Press in 1998.

Introduction

My love and devotion for horses started at a very early age. My parents supported me one hundred per cent and bought me my first pony when I was ten. I was a member of the Pony Club and the instruction I received from them gave me a solid foundation in both riding and stable management skills. At that time I competed regularly in affiliated show jumping competitions.

After leaving school I decided I wanted to pursue a full time career with horses. I came to The Yorkshire Riding Centre to train for the BHS qualifications. It was then that I developed a love for eventing. I was fortunate to be given a full time job as Christopher Bartle's competition groom, which has given me endless opportunities including grooming at top level dressage and eventing competitions. I also compete myself, producing young horses up to two star level. I have travelled to competitions around Europe and the USA, and have spent time riding and teaching in Australia and Jamaica.

I still work at The Yorkshire Riding Centre, where I enjoy competing and looking after the horses as much as ever. I also assist in the management of the yard and train students for competition and exams.

It is my aim in this book to pass on as much as possible of the specialist skills and knowledge which I have acquired during my career.

CHAPTER 1

Horse Health

As with humans all horses are different and should be treated as individuals. Knowing your horse is extremely important when it comes to recognizing that he is fit and healthy. Noticing a problem in the early stages will often prevent it becoming too serious.

It is your job as the groom to know what is normal for each individual horse both physically and psychologically. Anything abnormal for that horse, be it heat in a leg, a cough, loss of appetite or unusual behaviour should be reported to the rider before the horse is worked. Failing to recognize a problem early on and continuing to work a horse will often set him back a long way or cause more permanent damage. It is only over a period of time that you will fully get to know your horse; time must be spent looking and feeling over the body and legs to become familiar with normal lumps and bumps. Physically a horse alters as he gets fitter, he will change shape and the muscles will harden. The legs may become more filled as the work increases or they may tighten up with work. It is only when you have spent a full season with a horse that you will recognize what is normal for him.

As a horse gets older the legs will often show more permanent signs of wear and tear and this often makes it more difficult to recognize slight changes and new injuries. Many horses will change mentally as they get fitter, often becoming more stressed. This should not be ignored as psychological problems lead to physical problems and poor performance. Again, as a horse gets older he will change in his mental attitude, in my experience no two horses are ever the same. I had one horse who as a novice was very laid back, ate everything in sight, travelled well, and was a very easy horse to deal with, but as he got older and moved up the grades he became more stressed by competition, didn't travel as well, often going off his food and in general became much more uptight. A second horse, at Novice and Intermediate level was totally the opposite, he practically lived on fresh air as he wouldn't eat anything, he was very stressed when working at home and in competition, it was only the fact that he was so talented that we kept going with him. Now as a four star horse he is much more relaxed about everything, I actually have to keep him on a strict diet to control his weight.

The following are guide lines on what you should be looking for in a healthy horse. It is very important to be observant first thing in the morning as this is often when problems show.

BEHAVIOUR

- Bright and alert in and out of the stable.
- Reacts normally at feed time – most horses have their heads over the door looking eager to be fed, if he is standing at the back of the box uninterested it could indicate a problem.
- Shows his usual character when dealing with him – normal reactions when being mucked out, groomed and tacked up. If the usually friendly horse is uninterested or the usually grumpy, ears back type is suddenly happy for you to be around, it is often a sign he is 'off colour'.

APPETITE

- He should have eaten up previous feed (horses often go off feed when competitions start, do still check for other signs of illness).
- He is eating hay/haylage.
- Drinking – this can only be monitored if the horse has buckets. A sick horse or one that is known not to drink well should have his drinking monitored. Often a horse will stop drinking when under stress such as

travelling and at a competition; this can cause dehydration which will lead to physical problems and poor performance.

STABLE

- The bed looks normal for the horse.
- Droppings – normal amount and consistency.
- Urine – normal amount (should be light yellow colour).
- Check around the stable walls for new kick marks as these could be signs the horse has been cast.

DAILY CHECKS FOR INJURY OR ILL HEALTH

- Eyes – should be bright and free from discharge.
- Nose – clean and free from discharge, other than clear.
- Mouth – corners not cracked, bars not bruised. (Teeth are discussed later.)
- Head – no rubs from tack.
- Skin – should be supple, when pinched it should return to normal freely, if not it is a sign of dehydration. Always check for this after competitions, long journeys or strenuous training sessions. (See page 80 for dealing with dehydration). Free of disease.
- Coat – should lie flat and have a good shine, this should also apply to the grass-kept horse that is not being groomed.
- Condition – the horse should be a suitable weight for his age, type and work. Monitoring condition requires an experienced eye and often gradual changes are not recognized early enough. When caring for top competition horses it is useful to have other means of assessing condition such as a weigh bridge. (See page 91.) Overweight horses are as unhealthy as underweight ones and will be more susceptible to leg injuries when in training. An eye must also be developed for recognizing a 'lean' horse that is fit and a horse that is poor and carrying little condition. (See chapter 5 Feeding.)
- Legs – legs and feet should be checked first thing in the morning before the horse leaves the stable. Once the horse has worked it is more difficult

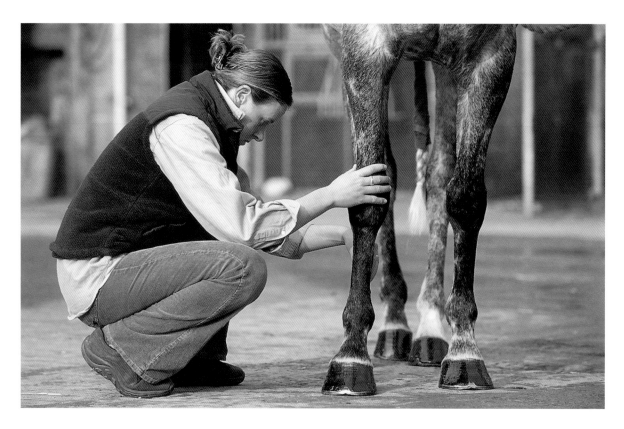

The legs must be checked carefully for heat, swelling and pain on pressure

to assess a problem as there will be heat in the limbs and swelling may be reduced. When assessing a problem after the horse has worked it is advisable to wait an hour to allow the feet and legs to cool down unless it is thought to be serious and needs immediate attention. Each leg should be felt for heat, swelling and pain on pressure. Without wearing gloves, run your hands slowly down each leg, paying particular attention to the knee, hock and lower leg as this is where most injuries occur.

The first sign of injury is heat and if you suspect slight heat in a leg compare to the other leg using the back of your hand as it is more sensitive to slight differences. Often in early stages or with minor injuries this is the only sign and because it isn't accompanied by swelling and lameness it is ignored and the horse continues to work causing further damage. Always react to the slightest change, remember the horse can't tell you how he is feeling. If heat or swelling is found apply pressure to the area, if the horse reacts it is likely he is sore in the area, he should then be trotted up to ascertain whether he is lame.

- Feet – check the temperature of each foot by feeling the wall of the hoof, ideally they should be cold, one hot foot often indicates a problem in the foot and it is usually accompanied by a strong digital pulse. When picking out the feet they should appear and smell healthy, special attention should be paid to the frog. Checks should also be made to the shoes and clenches.

No problem however slight should be ignored or it will get worse. Often when training for competition, riders don't want to believe they have a problem and don't stop working the horse until he is lame, this is often too late and serious damage has been done. If a problem is dealt with in the early stages it may mean missing a few competitions, ignoring it until the horse is lame may mean missing a full year or at worst never being able to compete at that level again.

All injuries are treated differently; an experienced person may suspect a bruise or knock and give the horse a few easy days. It is safer when in doubt or for the less experienced to have a vet assess the injury. The most important factor in the early stages with any injury is to reduce inflammation to aid the healing process and help prevent further damage. This can be done by applying ice or cold hosing until the vet arrives. In doing this it

Cold hosing a leg to reduce inflammation

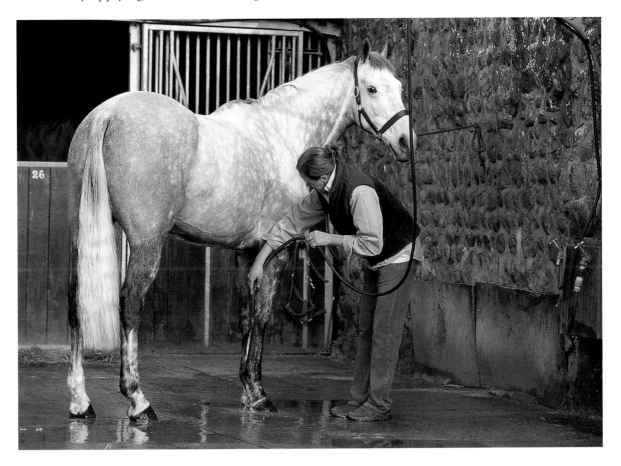

is important not to mask the injury therefore I would stop treating for an hour before the vet examines it unless it is very serious and obvious what the problem is.

Temperature/Pulse/Respiration

It is important to know the normal resting T.P.R for your horse as they give an accurate guide as to whether the horse is sick. To find an average they are taken every day for four days, it must be done at the same time of day in the same conditions. Ideally it should be taken first thing in the morning after the horse has eaten breakfast before he leaves the stable.

- Temperature – 37 to 38C (99.5 to 100.5F)
- Method – a regular human thermometer can be used or for the less experienced a digital one which is easier to read. An assistant is needed to hold the horse if he is unfamiliar with the procedure or known to be difficult, otherwise tie up.

The thermometer is inserted at a slight angle

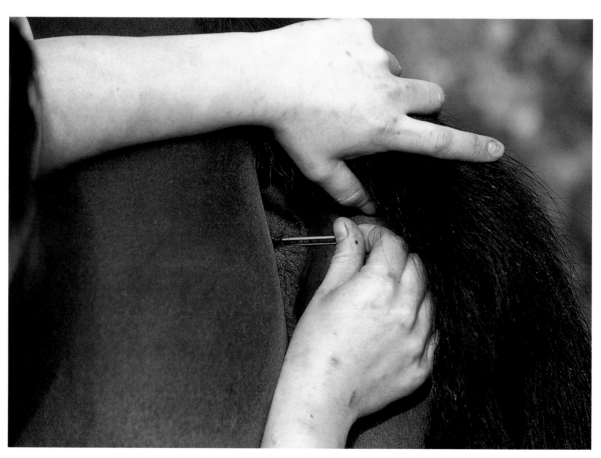

1. Check the thermometer is shaken down.
2. Stand behind the horse but slightly to the side close to the quarters.
3. The assistant can hold up a front leg on the same side as you are standing to prevent kicking.
4. Pull the tail to the side.
5. Insert the thermometer into the anal sphincter about three quarters of the way, slightly angle to the side to avoid putting it into faeces which would give a false reading.
6. Leave in for a minute. If the horse objects withdraw, never let go of the thermometer or risk it breaking inside.
7. Read and record.
8. Clean the thermometer and replace in case.

- Pulse – 30 to 40 beats per minute.
- Method – tie the horse up at the back of the box, he must be relaxed and not eating.
- There are two places which are fairly easy to find the pulse: under the jaw where the facial artery runs and the radial artery which is at the top, inside of the foreleg near the elbow.

Facial artery

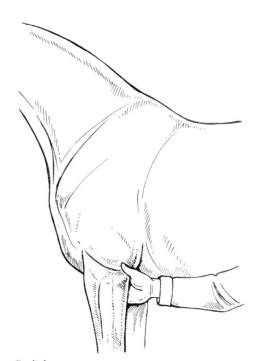

Radial artery

The pulse being taken

- Once the pulse is found count the beats for 30 seconds then double this to give the heart rate per minute.
- The alternative method is to use a stethoscope, placing it behind the left elbow.

- Respiration – 8 to15 breaths per minute.
- Method – the horse must be standing still and relaxed.
- Observe the flanks moving in and out as the horse breaths, each in and out is counted as one.
- Time for 30 seconds counting the breaths then double to give the rate per minute.

TEETH

Taking care of your horse's teeth is very important if you want to get the best out of him. It is useful to have a good knowledge of the structure of the mouth and of how to age a horse. All horses develop sharp edges to the molar teeth as a result of the jaw action when grinding food. The teeth should be checked and treated every six to twelve months; it is advisable that this is done by a vet or a qualified and licensed equine dentist.

If you suspect your horse has sharp teeth you can check by opening the mouth and holding the tongue, run your fingers along the outer edge of the upper pre-molars, sharp edges and points will be felt very easily. Of course I would not recommend someone without experience doing this. It is important to have a qualified equine dentist to check the mouth and carry

The equine dentist checks the molars for sharp edges

out treatment because to carry out a thorough inspection of the mouth it is necessary to apply a gag to keep the mouth open and be able to see and feel to the very back of the mouth. Beware of so called 'horse dentists' who arrive with a couple of rasps and take ten minutes to do the job, all they are doing is smoothing off the pre-molars. To do a thorough job it is necessary to use the gag to assess the mouth for problems and get to the very back.

Signs that the teeth may be causing problems

- Loss of appetite
- Difficulty chewing
- Quidding (dropping partially chewed food)
- Loss of condition
- Swellings on the jaw
- Abrasions to the tongue and gums
- Poor performance

A qualified dentist using the correct equipment

When to treat

Ideally have the teeth checked before the horse starts his competition season, often when a horse has had a problem in his mouth it will take a while for him to forget it and performance will not improve immediately after the cause has been removed, a holiday is a good time for him to forget. They should then be checked every six months.

Avoid having the dentist the day before a competition as the mouth may be sore, some more complicated treatments or difficult horses may require the vet to sedate them, this must be done at least ten days prior to competition due to the withdrawal date on the drugs.

WORMING

All horses have worms and no matter how well cared for still require regular worming, failure to do so could lead to ill health and poor performance and even, in extreme cases, death.

Symptoms

- Poor condition (often ribs showing and pot belly)
- Loss of appetite
- Dull coat
- Diarrhoea
- Tail rubbing
- Anaemia
- Poor performance
- Colic

The worming programme you follow will depend on the type of wormer you choose to use, when selecting a brand it is important it is effective in killing the following worms at all stages of its life cycle.

- Large redworm
- Small redworm
- Roundworm
- Pinworm

- Lungworm
- Threadworm
- Tapeworm
- Bots

There are several brands of wormer available, some more effective against certain worms than others, it is usual to use two brands throughout the year to be effective against all worms.

Example

- Worm with EQUEST every thirteen weeks
- Worm with EQUITAPE every six months. This is as well as EQUEST not instead of.

Any new horse that comes on to the yard should be wormed unless you can be sure it has been on a strict programme and it is advisable to do so before the horse is turned out and to keep stabled for forty-eight hours after worming.

During the competition season avoid worming the day before competition because occasionally worming can cause colic. I try to worm the evening before the horse has a day off.

Administering wormer

The most common method is to administer the wormer orally, most wormers come in a paste or gel that is easy to syringe into the back of the mouth.

METHOD

- Read the instructions enclosed in the box. Have the wormer ready, set at the quantity you intend to give. Place it in your pocket.
- Put a headcollar on the horse.
- Check that the horse's mouth is empty. It is not advisable to try to worm while the horse is eating as the wormer tends to get stuck to a ball of half chewed food which the horse then spits out.
- Stand beside the horse with your arm gently around his nose.
- Insert the wormer into the corner of the mouth aiming to the back of the mouth – not straight out of the other side!

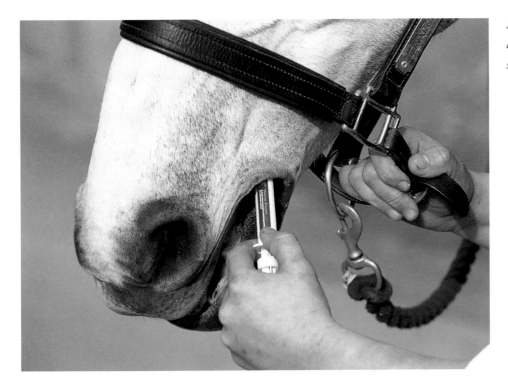

- Once given remove the syringe but keep the horse's head raised until he has swallowed and massaging the throat will encourage him to do so.

Some horses are very difficult to worm and it doesn't help to get angry with the horse but patience is necessary, it may help to use an empty syringe to get the horse used to it being put in the mouth and avoids wasting wormer which proves expensive. Combine this with rewarding the horse with a carrot or Polo mint so he learns to associate it with something he likes.

Another option is to mix the wormer into the feed, the horse may recognize the smell and want to eat it, mix with sugarbeet or molasses to disguise it and give as a last feed and leave in over night, the horse will often eat it when he gets hungry. Always remember to check the next morning.

If all methods fail it is possible to have the vet inject the drug.

VACCINATIONS

There are several vaccinations available to our horses to help keep them in good health, some are more important to certain horses than others. The two most important ones to the competition horse are tetanus and equine influenza.

Tetanus

Tetanus is a very serious disease; it is caused by the bacteria *Clostridium tetani* which is found in soil. If this gets into an airless situation such as a puncture wound it produces toxins and these affect the nervous system and if not treated will result in a prolonged and painful death.

All horses are susceptible to cuts and wounds and should be vaccinated against tetanus; this must be administered by the vet and consists of two intramuscular injections initially to be given no less than twenty-one days apart and no more than ninety-two. A third injection is then necessary no less than 150 days and no more than 215 days after the second injection. Booster injections are then given every two years.

Equine influenza

It is recommended for horses that are travelling and coming into contact with other horses to be vaccinated against equine influenza. Certain competition disciplines also require the horse to be fully vaccinated before registering. When stabling away for competition it is the policy of some yards that all horses entering are vaccinated and you may be asked to produce your vaccination certificate before entering the yard. The flu vaccine is given as the tetanus for the first three injections, the booster is then required annually. It is most common that the 'flu and tet' are given together as one injection; the horse then requires flu or flu/tet on alternate years.

Timing

It is best if the vaccination is given during a quiet period whilst the horse is on holiday, obviously this isn't always possible so careful planning should be made around the horse's competition and work programme. The vaccine could cause the horse to be off colour for up to a week after the injection and the horse should avoid being stressed. Some competition disciplines rule that the horse can not compete for seven days after the injection has been given.

KEEPING RECORDS

Health records should be kept for each horse to help you remember worming, vaccinations, teeth etc. Health problems and lameness should also be recorded as it is easy to forget minor problems but they are often the start of more serious problems. If the vet has to be called he will want an accurate history of the horse. How you choose to record information will depend on how many horses there are in your care and the facilities available to you. For one horse owners or small yards a diary or filing system is sufficient, for larger yards it may be easier to store information on computer.

Records to keep

VACCINATIONS
- Certificates kept updated and stored in a safe place. When competing it may be necessary to take certificates to the competition, it is useful to keep them in a folder to prevent them getting crumpled and dirty.
- Have a system to remind you two weeks in advance that a vaccination is due. The vet will need to be arranged and it may affect the training programme. If you have a filing system that is arranged monthly, check during the last week of each month which horses are due the following month, then work out a suitable date for it to be done and write in your yard diary when the vet is to be arranged.

TEETH
- Date done.
- Comments (often the dentist provides a report).
- How the horse reacted (for example if the horse was difficult assistance may be required next time).
- Date due for next check.

WORMING
- Date done.
- Type of wormer.
- Method of administering/how the horse reacted.

- After effects, if any.
- Date next due and type of wormer.

ILLNESS/LAMENESS

- Symptoms.
- If the vet was involved/ vet's name.
- Treatment.
- Medication.

VET VISITS

- All vet visits should be recorded in detail.

PHYSIOTHERAPY

- Date.
- Comments (the physiotherapist often gives a report).
- Treatment.
- After care.
- Improvements/changes in horse.

FIRST AID KIT

All horse owners should have a suitable first aid kit, it should contain essential equipment required for basic first aid or dealing with problems until the vet arrives. There are legal requirements on what we can store and administer ourselves and what must be done by the vet. The kit should be stored ideally in the tack room in a dry safe place. The following is a suitable first aid kit for a large yard, the quantity of equipment will obviously vary depending on the number of horses in your care. A separate kit will be needed for travelling and this is in chapter 8.

- Clean stable bandages
- Clean fibregee/cotton wraps
- Crepe bandages
- Equiwrap/vetwrap
- Equiplast

- Superflex
- Absorbent dressings – various sizes
- Robinson Activate carbon dressing
- Melolin
- Gamgee
- Cotton wool
- Ear buds
- Elastoplast roll
- Cling film
- Animalintex poultice
- Kaolin poultice
- Hibiscrub
- Pevadine
- Hexocil
- Savlon cream/spray
- Proflavin cream
- Dermobion
- Fuciderm
- Green oils
- Cleansing cream
- Intrasite gel
- Chloramphenicol eye ointment
- Tetcin spray
- Arnica gel/cream/pills
- Surgical spirit
- Witch hazel
- Disinfectant
- Epsom salts
- Table salt/ saline solution
- Vaseline
- Lip salve
- Bonjella
- Sun screen
- Fly repellent
- Ice tight
- Electrolytes

- Thermometers
- Scissors – various sizes, half curved
- Stethoscope
- Twitch
- Syringes – various sizes
- Tweezers
- Sterile bowl
- Sterile bucket
- Tubbing bucket
- Equiboot
- Cool packs/cool boots/ice bags
- Disposable gloves
- Clean towels
- Disposable cloths
- Tape
- Hoof pick

IMPORTANT TELEPHONE NUMBERS

The following numbers should be displayed in the tack room.

- Vet
- Farrier
- Dentist
- Physiotherapist
- Doctor
- Local police

CHAPTER 2

Care of the Foot and Shoeing

In my experience the saying 'no foot no horse' could not be truer. The foot is the most common cause of lameness. This can be due to poor conformation, neglect of the foot or bad shoeing. When buying a horse the first thing I look at is the conformation and condition of the feet, if this is poor and I feel little could be done to improve it I go no further. I work very closely with my farrier to ensure I take the best possible care and attention of the feet.

FOOT BALANCE

Good foot balance is essential if we are to keep our horses sound and performing to a high standard. The aim is to create equal weight distribution across the weight-bearing surfaces of the hoof; in return the joints, tendons and ligaments will be equally loaded and have the support they require.

Getting to know each individual horse's feet is important. It is often difficult to recognize slight changes in the early stages. As part of monitoring soundness your horse should be trotted up at least once a week. Observe the horse in walk and take time to look at each foot. The farrier should also be encouraged to assess the horses' action before shoeing if he suspects a problem.

Causes of foot inbalance

- Poor conformation of the foot and/or limbs
- Neglect
- Poor shoeing
- Injury
- Nutritional

Signs of inbalance

The feet should be viewed individually and as a pair. It is normal for the front feet to be a different size and shape to the hind feet.

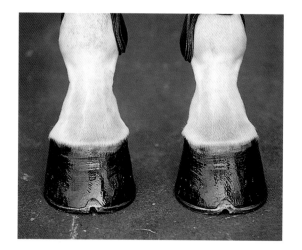

A good pair of front feet

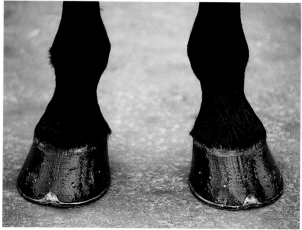

Feet turning out

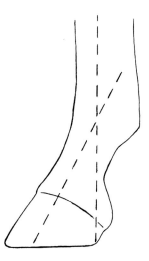

Correct hoof pattern axis

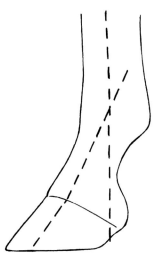

Broken back

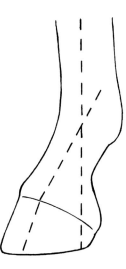

Broken forward

- Feet not a pair (size and shape).
- Poor hoof pastern axis. In my experience broken back is more of a problem as it is accompanied by long toes, low heels which then puts more strain on the superficial flexor tendon and suspensory ligament.
- Change in shape of feet due to uneven weight distribution. The horse should be viewed walking away and towards you. The foot should make contact with the ground evenly – not outside to inside or visa versa. If this can not be seen signs to check for are:
    - Uneven wear of the shoes.
    - Uneven hoof growth. The wall receiving more impact will grow faster and steeper. The side receiving less load will develop a flare.
    - Uneven heels.
    - Change in action.
    - Poor performance.
    - Lameness.

CARE OF THE FOOT

However good the foot is it still requires daily care and attention if it is to remain in good condition.

- The feet should be picked out at least twice daily. This should be done first thing in the morning and when the horse is finished off for the night. I would also advise picking out after work or turnout as mud and school surfaces packing the feet create an ideal environment for bacteria to thrive. This will lead to problems such as thrush.
- The feet may need scrubbing on the inside if the frog is becoming smelly. It is best done using warm water and a stiff brush. The water can contain anti-bacterial or fungal solution. Iodine will help to dry the foot if it has become too moist.
- The wall of the hoof should be scrubbed to allow thorough examination and before competition to improve appearance.

Recognizing problems

The first sign of injury or a problem in the foot is heat. Ideally the hoof wall should feel cool, especially when checked first thing in the morning. If all feet are warm this is likely to be normal. One hot foot usually indicates a problem.

The inside of the foot should neither be dry and brittle or moist and spongy. The frog should not smell offensive nor secrete a discharge. The hoof pick should be checked for this.

Hoof condition

Some horses have naturally strong, healthy feet. Others have poor, brittle feet. The essential factors to promote healthy growth are:

- Balanced diet.
- Regular foot trimming.
- Correctly fitted shoes.
- Training on good surfaces to reduce concussion.

Problems may still occur if the horse has naturally poor feet or is predisposed to certain conditions. Feet suffer either from standing in very wet conditions when they become very soft or very dry conditions as it affects the moisture level in the foot. As the foot dries out it becomes less able to cope with the demands of concussion and the wall will often crack. This makes nailing on the shoes difficult.

HOOF PRODUCTS

There are many topical products available to treat the feet and also to enhance the foot's appearance. Poor quality feet cannot be corrected by only applying topical products. However certain products can help prevent the loss of internal moisture. Others cause more problems by dehydrating the foot.

Supplements can be added to the diet to improve the quality of horn. Biotin is the most common supplement used. Oral and topical products will not be effective unless accompanied by good nutrition, shoeing and care of the feet.

RECOGNIZING WHEN A HORSE NEEDS SHOEING

It is commonly said a horse needs shoeing every six weeks. This would be average for a horse with good feet in moderate work. Horses out of work may go longer. Horses in hard work or with problem feet may need shoeing more frequently. Hoof growth is also slower during winter months.

Signs to check for

The shoes should be checked daily for the following when picking out the feet.

- Lost shoe/loose shoe.
- Twisted shoe.
- Risen clenches – these should be knocked down until the farrier is called as they could cause injury to the opposite leg.
- The foot has become long or out of balance.

Checking the feet after shoeing

- The horse should be trotted up immediately after shoeing to check he is sound.
- Ensure the correct type of shoe has been fitted.
- Check that there are the correct number of stud holes if required.
- Ensure stud holes are tapped.
- Check that there are road studs or grip if required.

STUD HOLES

Horses that are competing on grass in dressage, show jumping or cross country will require stud holes. Studs can then be screwed in at the competitions to give the shoes more grip in slippy conditions. (See page 170.)

It is most common to have two stud holes, one at each heel of the shoe. Some may only require one on the outside heel of the shoe. Often show jumpers have more as they require ultimate grip when turning tight against the clock. Care of the stud holes is essential if they are to last as long as the shoes.

Cleaning

- The holes should be cleaned out the day before the competition after the horse has worked. It can be time consuming if the holes have stones in them, this can be difficult to deal with at the competition if working in the confines of a horse box or your horse is excited. Use a sharp object such as a nail or bradall to remove the dirt and stones.
- Spray the hole with WD 40.
- Use the tap to clean the threads. It is very easy to cross the threads if this is not done with care. The tap should turn easily and should never be forced.
- Plug the hole with cotton wool soaked in baby oil.
- At the competition it should be easy to remove the plug and screw the stud in. If the stud doesn't go in easily it may be necessary to use the tap again. The more the tap is used the quicker the threads will wear so don't use it unnecessarily.

SPARE SHOES

Shoes are often lost during competition especially on the cross-country. A farrier is often available to replace lost shoes and it is much easier and cheaper if you can provide your own shoes. When competing in three-day events it is essential to have a spare set of shoes for your horse. If a shoe is lost on the steeplechase it must be replaced as quickly as possible. It is a serious disadvantage if the farrier has to find a shoe that fits.

I prefer to use a set of shoes that my horse has worn rather than a new set. At the beginning of the season I take a set of shoes that are in good enough condition to refit, making sure that they have the correct number of stud holes and the threads are in good order, if not the farrier can put new stud holes in.

When shoeing prior to a three-day event I often take the shoes that have come off him as my spares as these will be the closest fit to his feet. If these are not suitable and you intend to use an older spare set have the farrier check they still fit the horse as his feet may have changed size or shape.

Horses that are shod with bar shoes may have to change into open heeled shoes during the competition if conditions become very wet. Bar shoes tend to be pulled off in the mud. In this case it is necessary to carry two sets of spare shoes – one to put on the horse and a spare set.

TIMING OF SHOEING IN RELATION TO COMPETITION

Consideration must be made as to when it is ideal to shoe your horse in relation to your competition. Some horses are not affected at all by shoeing, others can be shorter in their action for a few days. There is also the slight chance the farrier may make a mistake and over trim or prick the horse causing lameness. The horse will also need time to adjust to any major changes in foot balance.

If the horse is competing most weekends and does become short after shoeing have him shod early in the week so he has time to recover. For three-day events the horse must pass a trot up so, to be on the safe side, I tend to have them shod ten days before.

FARRIER RELATIONS

It is important to be able to discuss your horses' feet with your farrier. You see the feet everyday and know how he is performing. Any slight changes should be reported to the farrier on his next visit or sooner if it is more serious. The problems should be pointed out and discussed and the farrier allowed to make his own judgement. It is not advisable to try to tell him how to do his job. For more serious problems it may be necessary for the vet to assess the condition, he will then work with the farrier advising on foot balance and corrective shoeing.

SHOEING RECORDS

- Date of shoeing.
- What was done – for example, new shoes, refits, type of shoe, stud holes.
- Farrier's comments – condition of feet, changes in balance.
- Date of next appointment.

CHAPTER 3

Grooming and Turnout

Daily grooming is very important because it gives you the opportunity to check that the horse is healthy. During this time you need to thoroughly check over skin, coat, legs and feet. Regular grooming also enables you to promote healthy skin and coat condition, improve circulation and muscle tone and of course improve the horse's appearance.

Items of the grooming kit

THE GROOMING KIT

GROOMING KIT BOX

There are many available which vary in design and price. If travelling and working outside it is advisable to have a box with a lid to keep your kit dry and clean. A box sturdy enough to stand on comes in useful when plaiting.

DANDY BRUSH

Used on heavy coats to remove mud and sweat. Sensitive, clipped or fine-coated horses may not like the use of the firm bristles and care should be taken when used on head and legs. This type of brush is also useful for scrubbing the inside and outside of the hooves.

BODY BRUSH

Used on all areas to remove dirt and grease. Available in various sizes and designs, the most effective and comfortable for groom and horse are the leather-backed type.

FLICKY BRUSH

Recently introduced, I don't think any groom should be without one. It is a soft long bristled brush useful for quartering, removing dust and dampening manes and tails

METAL CURRY COMB

Used to remove dirt and grease from the body brush.

RUBBER CURRY COMB

Used to remove hair from moulting horses and to bring dirt and grease to the surface of the coat.

PLASTIC CURRY COMB

This is often used on manes and tails but this is not advisable as it will pull out a lot of hair. It can be used to remove mud and dry sweat from the coat and I prefer it to the rubber curry comb. Many horses enjoy the use of it as a form of massage, or to give a good scratch to stabled horses that wear a lot of rugs and don't have the chance to roll.

SPONGES

At least two to wash eyes, nose, dock and for removing stable stains.

HOOF PICK

It is advisable to have two per grooming kit as this enables you to carry one with you at a competition and is also a safeguard in case one is lost.

The above covers the basic grooming kit, for more professional care and turnout other accessories are needed.

PLAITING/TRIMMING

For plaiting and trimming the following additional items will be required.

COMBS
Large plastic or metal
Small pulling comb
Small human plastic comb cut to size to apply quarter markings

SCISSORS
Large for trimming
Small for plaiting

PLAITING THREAD
Various colours

PLAITING BANDS
Various colours

NEEDLES
Large, blunt

CLIP OR CLOTHES PEG
To separate mane when plaiting

RAZORS

For shaving whiskers

SMALL BATTERY HAND CLIPPERS

TAIL BANDAGE

LARGE SPONGES

SWEAT SCRAPER

SHAMPOO

COAT SHINE/MANE AND TAIL CONDITIONER

BABY OIL

CHALK

TALCUM POWDER

HOOF OIL/BRUSH

METHODS OF GROOMING

There are several methods of grooming all of which are effective in checking, cleaning and improving the turnout of the horse. Each method is effective in cleaning different types of coat, consideration must also be taken into the amount of time available for grooming each horse.

Thorough grooming

To be carried out on fit, healthy stabled horses, I find it much easier if the horse is tied up whilst being groomed. I prefer to do it after exercise so the horse is finished off for the day feeling clean and comfortable. It is more

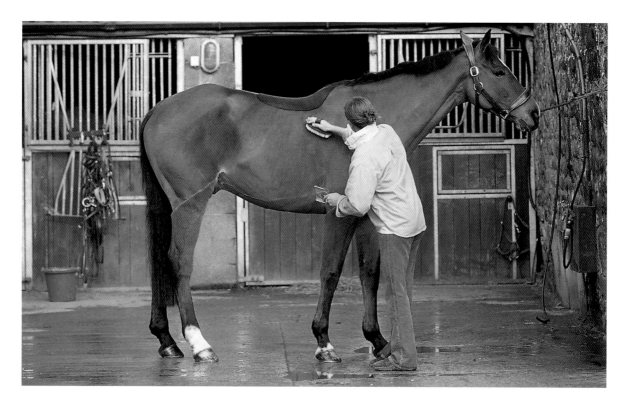

A horse being groomed using the body brush and curry comb

effective to groom a horse that is slightly warm as the pores will be open, however a very hot or sweaty horse will need to cool and dry first. This is not suitable for grass-kept, sick or tired horses.

Pick out the feet, checking condition of the foot, it should appear and smell healthy. Check condition of shoes and clenches.

- Scrub the feet inside and out.
- Use a plastic or rubber curry comb on the neck and body areas. This is not necessary on horses which have been clipped.
- With the body brush start with the mane, separate and brush underneath, then groom the neck, body and legs using the metal curry comb to keep the brush clean. Never wear gloves when grooming as it is important to run your hands over each area checking for swelling, heat or pain on pressure. If you groom the same horse each day you will recognize how the horse reacts to each area and what lumps and bumps are normal. Anything new needs further attention as it may be an early sign of soreness, ill fitting tack or injury. If the horse is suddenly objecting to being groomed in a certain area that he is usually happy with, he is telling you he is in pain and this should be investigated.

The horse should be untied to brush the head

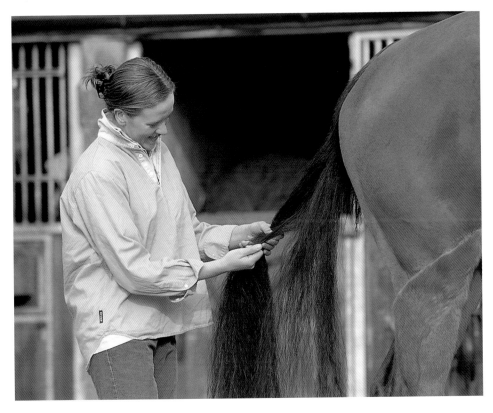

The fingers can be used to separate the tail to avoid loss of hair

When grooming your horse there are some areas which require special attention and these are as follows.

The *head* – especially the corners of the mouth behind the ears and where the noseband fits. The *back* – especially the saddle area, the withers and the girth. The *shoulders* which can often be rubbed by rugs. The *legs and feet* from knee and hock down.

When grooming the head use the body brush. It is advisable to untie the horse first. Special attention should be paid behind the ears and under the jaw where the horse may sweat a lot.

Avoid brushing the tail too frequently and not on a daily basis as it will thin very quickly. The top of the tail can be brushed with the body brush, separating each area to get to the dock. The bottom of the tail can be separated by using your fingers to remove bedding and prevent pulling out the hair. Never use the dandy brush, plastic curry combs or combs on the tail. I wash the tail weekly or before a competition, then apply tail conditioner which makes it easier to manage. I then use my fingers to remove bedding and work out the tangles when necessary.

Separate sponges should be used for the eyes, nose and dock and a small piece of cloth such as a tea towel is ideal to use as a stable rubber to give a final wipe over the horse.

Quartering

The term 'quartering' is used to describe a quick groom and means that the rugs are not totally removed but quartered forward and back as each area is done. The aim of quartering is to make the horse look presentable for work and at the same time to check him over. It is usually done in the morning or prior to exercise.

The main points when quartering are to:
- Pick out the feet, making the same checks as when grooming.
- Flick the horse off by using the body or flicky brush, removing obvious dirt and stable stains, checking each area as you go along.
- Brush over and lay the mane.
- Remove bedding from the tail.
- Brush the head.
- Sponge eyes, nose and dock.

- Damp the top of the tail and apply a tail bandage.
- Re-do rugs as necessary.
- Sponge off stable stains (especially on grey horses).
- Use a damp brush to lay the coat of thick-coated horses.

Hot clothing

Hot clothing is a useful method of cleaning clipped or very fine-coated horses. To do this you will require:

Half bucket of very hot water

Rubber gloves

Cloth or sponge

Place the cloth into the hot water then thoroughly squeeze out, starting at the neck scrub the skin with the hot damp cloth, this is repeated over the body, legs and head, frequently dipping into the hot water. As well as cleaning the coat the heat will also open the pores, this can be followed by grooming with the body brush. Care should be taken on cold days not to allow the horse to get chilly; to avoid this, rugs can be folded as for quartering. This is a much quicker method than a thorough groom and is very effective on clipped horses.

Bathing

It is more practical to bath a horse in hot weather than to give a thorough groom. It is more effective if done immediately after exercise when the horse is hot or sweating. Depending on weather conditions warm or cold water can be used, never use very hot water as the horse will feel much colder afterwards. There are many shampoos on the market but these can be very expensive, often grey horses need a suitable shampoo to remove stains but I find a mild human shampoo just as effective on other coats and much cheaper. If shampoo is used too frequently it removes the natural oils from the skin and leaves the coat looking dull. Using shampoo once a week is adequate, water on its own can be used to wash a sweaty horse off, followed by a quick brush off when dry.

BATHING IN COLD WEATHER

It is sometimes necessary to bath a horse in cold weather, especially preparing a grey horse for competition. It is important to keep the horse as warm as possible whilst doing this. The key things when doing this are as follows:

- Have all equipment needed ready including suitable rugs, stable bandages and towels.
- Have easy access to warm water or an assistant to keep buckets topped up.
- Start with the tail as this can be done with the rugs still on. After rinsing, plait and tie up to keep clean.
- Fold the rugs back, wash the mane and neck area. Rinse, scrape and towel dry. Drape a cooler over the neck.
- Fold the rugs back to the quarters, repeat the process. Don't worry about legs at this stage.
- Fold the rugs forward and do the same to the hind quarters. The horse can then be rugged up with suitable coolers; Thermatex rugs are very useful for drying and keeping the horse warm. If the horse is cold it may be necessary to hand walk, horse walk or lunge, warm the horse before washing the legs and head.
- Pick out and scrub the feet inside and out. Wash, rinse and thoroughly towel dry the legs. Stable bandages can be applied to keep the legs dry and clean.
- Untie the horse to wash the head. Care should be taken not to get soap and water into the eyes and ears. After rinsing towel dry the face.
- Manes and tails should be brushed through and laid.
- Once dry, clean rugs should be applied, hoods also help to keep the neck clean.

Grooming heavy coats

Not all horses are clipped throughout the winter, for example young horses or horses in light work. It may be necessary at some point to have the horse looking smart. Grooming heavy coats on a daily basis will improve condition and appearance, it is also very important to thoroughly check the horse as problems can easily be missed under a thick coat so use your hands to check the condition by feeling how much covering is over the ribs. After grooming, appearance is improved if a damp brush is run over the coat followed by a dry cloth. A well pulled mane and tail, trimmed feathers and whiskers will also improve appearance.

Grooming machines

Grooming machines are effective in doing the job of thorough grooming and can be labour saving. Ideally the machine is set up in a box ready to use and horses are taken to the box to be groomed. This system works well on larger yards, otherwise setting the machine up each time can be time consuming. There are several types on the market but all are expensive not making it economical for one horse owners or small yards. They are also useful to use on young horses to prepare them for clipping.

Grooming the grass-kept horse

Horses that are living out should not be groomed in the same way as the stabled horse as the natural oils in the coat protect from cold and rain. It is still important to check the horse daily by running the hands over the body and legs, particular attention should be paid to the back and hindquarters for signs of rain scald and the legs and belly for mud fever and cracked heels. The feet should be picked out on a regular basis. If the horse is being ridden the worst of the mud can be removed with a dandy brush, rubber or plastic curry comb.

Grooming the sick or injured horse

As with people a horse that is in pain or suffering from a virus will not appreciate being fussed over. Therefore just the basics should be done - feet picked out, rugs adjusted, eyes, nose and dock kept clean.

Grooming tired horses

A horse that is tired after hunting or competition should be dealt with as above. Hunters can be bathed immediately on return if suitable facilities are available using hot water and heat lamps. Alternatively remove the heavy mud and sweat and groom the following day.

Coat products

There are several proprietary brands that are useful to apply to the coat after bathing to give shine. Avoid areas where tack fits as it often makes the coat very slippery causing equipment to move. They can be helpful to use before or during competition as they prevent dust settling on the coat. They should not be used as a substitute for grooming.

Mane and tail products

Never apply any of these to the mane if you are plaiting as it will make the mane extremely slick and impossible to keep the plait tight. They are useful to use on tails to help keep them tangle-free and their use makes it much easier to remove bedding. They should be applied after washing.

TRIMMING

Pulling the mane

Manes should be pulled every two to three weeks. A well pulled mane improves appearance, keeps it out of the way when riding, and is easier and quicker to plait. The ideal length depends on the thickness of the hair and whether or not the mane is to be plaited. Often a shorter mane is easier to plait but may not lie as well when not plaited giving an untidy appearance, therefore pull the mane to suit the horse and make your job easier.

It is more comfortable to pull the mane when the horse is warm from exercise especially in winter. It is also easier to pull a greasy mane rather than a freshly washed mane that is very slick.

Methods of pulling

COMB

The most suitable comb to use is the small, narrow, metal comb. I usually start in the centre of the mane as I find the horse least sensitive here.

- Take a small amount of mane from underneath between finger and thumb.
- Take the comb in the other hand; take excess mane away by combing upwards towards the crest leaving about twenty hairs in your hand.

The comb is used to separate the hair

A small amount of hair is wrapped around the comb

- Wrap the hair around the comb.
- Pull the mane out by a quick downward movement.
- This is repeated along the mane, frequently combing the mane down to check the length and thickness.
- This process is the most effective and suitable for most manes and horses that are not too sensitive.

FINGERS

The mane can be pulled by using your fingers only. This method is suitable for very thin manes, or for horses that will not tolerate the comb method.

- Take a very small amount of mane from underneath between two fingers.
- Pull downwards and quickly.

This method is very slow and not suitable for long or very thick manes.

THICK/LONG MANES

If the mane has got very long it is often easier to cut before pulling. Work out how short you intend the mane to be before you start as pulling it will shorten as well as thin.

Thick manes are more difficult to deal with, especially if they are to be plaited. Thin the mane as much as possible using the comb method, often it cannot be done all at once as the horse becomes too sore. It is better that a thick mane is pulled more frequently. If the mane is to be plaited I find it easier if it is left a little longer than normal.

THIN MANES

It can be a problem pulling a thin mane short enough without making it too thin for plaiting. I find using the finger method preferable to the comb.

DEALING WITH DIFFICULT HORSES

Not all horses are tolerant of having their manes pulled and often an assistant is needed to help. Different methods of restraint can be applied, I often find putting on a twitch the best way as it stops the horse getting wound up and enables you to get the job done quickly. Not all horses however react in the desired way to the twitch and it makes matters worse and often dangerous. Applying oil of cloves to the crest has a mild anaesthetic effect and may help, gloves must be worn to do this. Very difficult horses require a lot of patience and often pulling is not an option but other methods can be used.

CUTTING

Cutting the mane gives a very unnatural appearance, however this is often the only solution with very difficult horses and recently has become a popular look in the show jumping circuit. It is very quick and easy to do using a large pair of scissors and can look tidy if the mane is laid over neatly.

SCISSORING

Scissoring is a method of cutting without giving the blunt appearance. It can be done on horses that don't tolerate the mane being pulled or for a thin mane that needs shortening without thinning. The scissors need to be large and sharp, the mane is cut length ways rather than across until the desired length and thickness is achieved.

Pulling the tail

A pulled tail gives a much more tidy appearance especially for horses that are competing. A tail that is to be plaited for competition must be left 'full'. Horses tend to be more sensitive to having their tails pulled and as you are standing behind the back legs care should be taken.

METHOD

The hair is pulled from under and down the side of the dock, starting at the top of the tail, finishing 20 to 25cm (8 to 10in)down depending on the horse's conformation. Avoid taking too much hair from the middle of the tail although with very thick tails it is necessary. The hair can be pulled using the comb method but I find this takes out too much hair at once and prefer to use my fingers.

The dock will become sore very quickly and often bleeding is visible, so when pulling a 'full' tail for the first time it is best done over a period of days. Once the tail is pulled it can be kept tidy by doing it once a week. A common problem is pulling out too much hair, giving a bald appearance down each side of the dock, this is avoided by not taking too much out at once and making sure it is done evenly. A well pulled tail takes practice and patience.

A well pulled tail

Horses that object to having their tails pulled may benefit from the oil of cloves. It is more difficult to restrain a horse safely when pulling the tail and to prevent getting kicked an assistant can hold the horse's head with his tail backed to a closed stable door and the tail can be pulled from outside the stable with the door to protect you.

I tend to avoid putting a tail bandage on a freshly pulled tail as it will irritate it if it is sore, however to make a pulled tail look neat it will need to be bandaged.

Trimming the tail

The length of tail is cut by using large, sharp scissors. Deciding how short to have the tail is personal preference and can often depend on what job the horse is doing. It is more practical for the hunter to have a short tail as it is frequently galloping through wet, muddy conditions. For the dressage and show horse consider the conformation of the hind leg, if it is poor it may be an advantage to leave the tail longer as a short tail may exaggerate the weakness. A pulled tail suits a shorter finish where a plaited tail looks better left slightly longer. Once the length is decided remember to consider how the horse carries the tail when working, if he has a high tail carriage it can make quite a difference and should not be cut too short.

METHOD

The tail needs to be thoroughly brushed through and tangle free, take the tail between finger and thumb keeping it as straight as possible, run the hand down to the desired length, turn upside down and cut along fingers, let the tail down to check on straightness, it may need a second cut to achieve a straight finish.

Trimming feathers

The feathers around the heels and back of fetlock joints should be trimmed on stabled horses to improve appearance, make grooming easier and to enable the legs to be checked more thoroughly.

METHOD

It is done by using a large plastic comb and a large pair of scissors. The reason for using the comb is to give a more natural cut to the hair and eliminate 'steps' in the cut. The horse should be tied up and be familiar with his legs

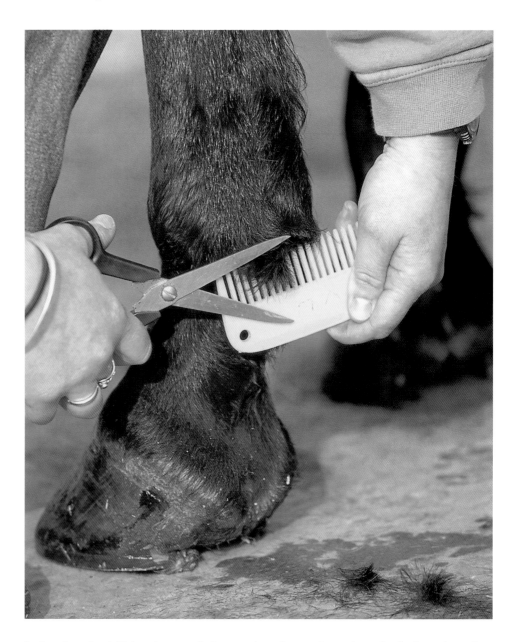

being brushed. Take the comb in one hand, comb against the hair so it pokes through the teeth, the hair is then cut with the scissors through the comb. This is repeated around the fetlock and heels until the excess hair is removed.

Another method is to use small hand clippers and this is much quicker. To give a more natural look clip down the hair rather than against it as this will remove excess feather without giving too close a shave.

It is not advisable to trim the feathers of horses that are living out in wet, muddy conditions as the feather will offer protection against cracked heels. It is also not suitable for some showing classes of native breeds.

Trimming the coronet band

To give a good finish to the leg the excess hair around the coronet band can be trimmed by using large sharp scissors. This gives a neat appearance and makes it much easier to apply hoof oil.

Trimming whiskers

Whether you choose to trim the whiskers or not is a personal choice, I think it makes the horse look much tidier, others may argue that the whiskers are there for a reason and the horse relies on them, this may be the case of the horse in the wild but I don't believe he needs them to find his food in the stable.

METHODS

SCISSORS – Cut the whiskers as close as possible using curved scissors. I find this very slow and there is a high risk of cutting the horse if he moves.
RAZOR – Use a sharp disposable razor, it helps if the area is wet. Most horses are happy to let you do this although care should be taken as the horse may try to grab the razor with his lips.
CLIPPERS – The whiskers can be removed when clipping the horse or with small hand clippers.

WHEN TO DO

The whiskers should be removed prior to competition, however some horses can become sensitive which is a problem in summer when flies and bugs are about. If the horse shows sensitivity I find it best to do this a few days prior to competition.

WHEN NOT TO DO

Having had experience with horses that are prone to head shaking I have found them to be much worse with their whiskers removed. Horses that are prone to this or who are sensitive around the nose are best left with the whiskers on.

Trimming under the jaw

This can be done by using the same comb and scissor method as described for trimming the feathers to give a more natural look. It can also be done by using small clippers, clipping in the direction of the hair. Often heavier coated horses need it during the summer or to tidy the head in winter if the horse hasn't been clipped.

Laying manes

There are several methods that are effective in laying a mane over to the correct side. This is done to give a more tidy appearance.

Laying the mane

METHODS

PLAITING OVER – The most popular and effective method is to plait the mane to train it to lie on the correct side. The mane should be brushed over to the right side of the neck; it is then divided and put into plaits which are secured by a rubber band, the plaits don't need to be too tight. The plaits can be left in for up to two days providing the horse doesn't try to rub them out. When the plaits are removed the mane should stay on the correct side, if not it may be necessary to repeat the exercise.

BUNCHES – This is similar to plaiting but not as effective with more difficult manes. The mane is brushed over to the correct side and divided up into bunches, again these can be left in for up to two days.

HOODS/NECK COVERS – Hoods, neck covers and blankets help to lay the mane over. It is of course important to check that the mane is on the correct side before they are put on and once on check again that the entire mane is over.

DAMPENING – A mane that is trained to lie on the correct side will benefit from a damp brush each day after grooming or quartering.

WHEN NOT TO PLAIT OVER – Horses that are prone to mane rubbing should not have plaits left in over night. It is also not advisable to leave plaits in when flies and midges are about as the mane offers some protection. Never leave plaits or bunches in horses that suffer from sweet itch.

Laying tails

A pulled tail will need to be bandaged for a few hours daily to keep it looking tidy. The top of the tail should be dampened before the bandage is applied. Do not put on a bandage too soon after pulling the tail as it may be sore and never leave a tail bandage on overnight.

Bridle paths

The bridle path is the area of mane where the headpiece of the bridle sits. It is personal preference as to whether you cut it or not, it can make putting the bridle on easier, especially if your horse is head shy around the ears. It can be cut by using scissors or small hand clippers.

PLAITING

Manes

Before plaiting the mane it should be pulled to a suitable length. The mane should be clean but it is often difficult to plait a freshly washed mane so I advise washing two days prior to plaiting.

Equipment

- Comb (large plastic or metal)
- Scissors
- Thread/Bands
- Butterfly clip
- Water brush

Choosing bands or thread to secure the plait is personal preference; bands are quicker but don't look as professional, suitable for hunting or show jumping. Thread gives a much neater finish and is more secure therefore more popular for eventing, dressage and showing.

METHOD

- Tie the horse up.
- Decide how much mane is going to be used for each plait and this will vary depending on length and thickness of mane. It is important that this remains constant down the neck so the plaits appear evenly spaced.
- Place an elastic band on the comb to give a guide as to the amount of mane for each plait.
- The mane can be divided and put into bunches but this does take more time.
- Use the comb to part the mane which will make it much neater.

Use the comb to divide the mane equally

- After separating the mane use a butterfly clip or clothes peg to keep the rest of the mane out of the way.
- Plait the mane down as tightly as possible; often a plait doesn't stay in because the initial plait was not tight enough.
- The bottom of the plait can then be secured by a band or thread, the bottom of the plait should be doubled up to prevent stray hairs sticking out when the plait is rolled up.

- The plait is then rolled into the neck to form a ball which is then secured with a band or thread.

A mane plaited using thread

METHODS OF SEWING

- Always use thick plaiting thread as close to the colour of the mane as possible.
- The needle should be large and blunt for safety.
- Tie a knot in the end of the thread.
- Plait the hair down and hold the end tight, bring the thread through from the back of the plait to the front, wrap once around the plait then thread through again, fold up the end and repeat to secure.
- Roll the plait up into the neck with the thread still attached.
- The plait can then be secured by sewing from back to front, wrapping the thread around one side of the plait then the other, repeated about three times. This secures it well but the thread is visible and it can loosen the shape of the plait. To make it neater sew from front to back without taking around the outside of the plait.

Plaiting the forelock

The forelock can be plaited using the same method as the mane or it can be done with a French plait. Hair is taken from each side and plaited into the centre, this method is more time consuming but looks more professional.

Plaiting to complement the horse

The number and size of plaits you do is personal preference, it can however have some influence on improving conformational faults. Traditionally they were always an uneven number but this is not something I worry about.

The plaits should complement the horse

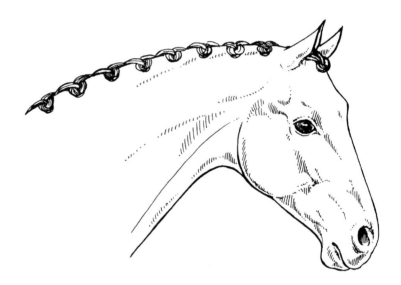

LONG NECK – The less plaits the better as more will exaggerate the length of neck. Cutting a long bridle path and trimming the mane at the wither also helps to shorten the appearance of the neck.

SHORT NECK – The opposite of the long neck, as many plaits as possible will help make the neck look longer.

WEAK TOP LINE – A horse with a poor neck or 'upside down' neck will improve by having large plaits set on top of the neck creating the impression the horse has more muscle on top.

How long to leave plaits in

It is often necessary to plait the horse the night before a competition; this should not be a problem unless the horse is prone to rubbing. Plaits can be left in for up to two days but I wouldn't advise longer than that.

When plaiting the night before I would recommend that the horse wears a hood to prevent bedding getting in the plaits and them becoming untidy. If the plaits have become untidy over night it may be necessary to trim stray hairs around the plait, be very cautious when doing so as the mane will thin very quickly, I tend to reserve this for important competitions. Hair spray or gel is another option to keep loose hairs under control.

Plaiting the tail

The horse must have a good full tail if it is to be well plaited. The tail needs to be clean and well brushed through, as with the mane I find it ideal to wash two days before.

METHOD

Tie the horse up.

- Starting as high as possible take a small piece of hair from each side of the dock, it is important that the same amount of hair is taken each time, the two pieces are crossed over at the centre of the dock.
- Take another piece from the side opposite to the piece you have on top, this gives you three pieces to plait with.
- Continue to plait down taking from alternate sides, it is important to keep the plait as tight as possible.
- The plait should finish approximately three quarters of the way down the dock. Finish the plait off to the bottom without adding more hair.
- Sew the end of the plait as with the mane, double the plait up and sew together.
- The plait should then be protected by a tail bandage and if travelling I would also recommend a tail guard.
- The tail must never be plaited the day before competition and left in all night as the horse is likely to rub it.

During summer months horses often rub the tail making plaiting more difficult. If the top of the tail has been rubbed a plaiting band can be used to help secure the start of the plait. Stray bits of hair can be trimmed and hair spray applied to help it stay in place.

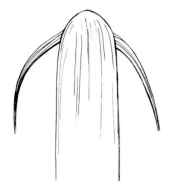

Take a small piece of hair from each side of the dock

Cross over at centre of tail. Take a third piece from each side

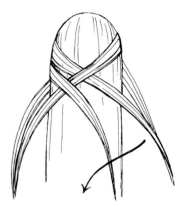

Continue to plait down taking hair from alternate sides

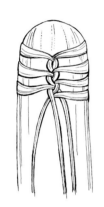

Sew the end of the plait as with the mane

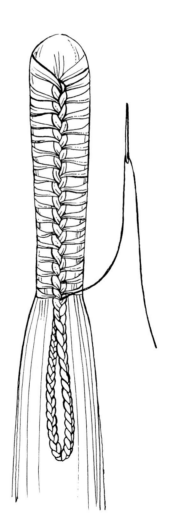

Double the plait up and sew together

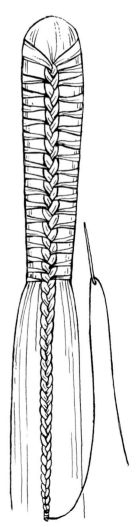

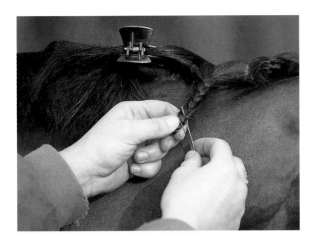

The bottom of the plait is secured

The plait is secured by sewing from the front to the back

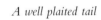

A well plaited tail

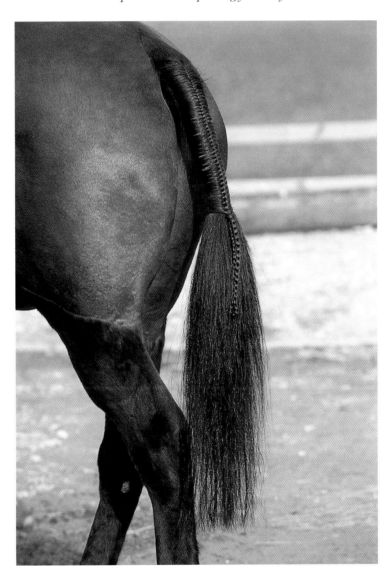

TURNOUT TIPS FOR COMPETITION/SHOW RING

The following are tips on final touches to turnout before the horse goes in the ring.

Body

Flick the neck and body off with a flicky brush followed by a wipe over with a dry cloth. If the coat is dull a small amount of coat shine can be applied and brushed into the coat, avoid the saddle area as it can cause the saddle to slip.

Quarter markings

Professionally applied on good shaped hind quarters can look very smart but done badly or on poor hindquarters can have an adverse effect.

The horse needs strong hind quarters and a good hindleg to carry the quarter markings well, they will draw attention to the area so it is important it is a strong point especially when showing or a dressage competition.

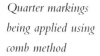

Quarter markings being applied using comb method

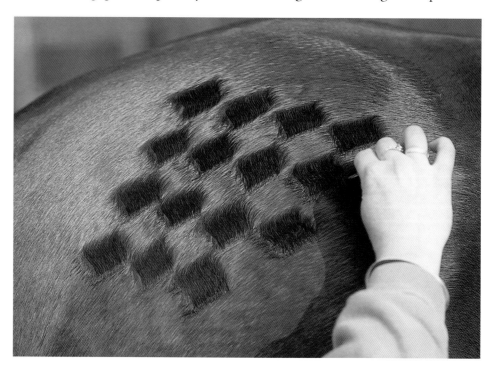

Choose the correct size and number for each individual horse, often they are over done which spoils the effect.

METHODS OF APPLYING

BRUSH – A firm, short bristled body brush is most effective. Wet the brush to apply the markings.

STENCIL – Use a wet brush to damp the area of coat, put the stencil in place, with a wet brush, brush over the stencil downwards so the hair is brushed in the wrong direction. Lift the stencil away.

COMB – A small hand comb needs to be cut to size. Use a wet body brush to damp the coat. Apply the markings by combing the hair in the wrong direction.

Quarter markings are usually accompanied by 'sharks' teeth'. To help prevent them being rubbed off apply hair spray to the coat. If fly spray is being used apply after the hairspray. In hot weather flies may be a pest and cause the horse to swish his tail, this could spoil the markings so they should be done at the last minute. On cold days the horse may need to wear a rug and to prevent it rubbing fold forward leaving the markings uncovered.

Legs

The legs should be brushed off and any stains removed, if the feet have got dirty they need to be washed before the socks. Black legs can be wiped over with a damp sponge followed by a dry towel. Baby oil can be applied to give extra shine. White legs can be chalked to cover any reluctant stains or to give an extra white finish, the chalk works best if the hair is slightly damp.

Mane

Remove all bedding or hay that may have got in over night or whilst travelling. Trim any stray hairs and apply hairspray to give extra hold.

Tail

Remove the tail bandage; unroll rather than pull off if the tail is plaited. Give a thorough brush and apply a small amount of baby oil to give extra shine.

If the tail is pulled wash the dock and damp the top of the tail, put the tail bandage back on until just before the horse goes in the ring. Apply a small amount of baby oil under the tail. The same can be done to a plaited tail as well as trimming the stray hairs and applying hairspray.

Face

Brush the face with the body or flicky brush, wipe the eyes, nose and mouth with a damp sponge. It is very important the horse is not eating at this stage as his mouth will become very messy once the bit is in. Any white markings can be chalked. Put a small amount of baby oil onto your hands and wipe around muzzle and eyes. Fly spray can be applied using your hands or a cloth.

Feet

Pick out the feet and brush the inside with a stiff brush. The outside of the hoof may need scrubbing, allow to dry then apply hoof oil to the inside and outside of the hoof. There are many types of hoof oil available, I prefer to use the thick black on black feet only, with white feet I prefer the thin hoof oil followed by a layer of baby oil to give extra shine.

CHAPTER 4
Clipping

There are several reasons why horses are clipped and these include allowing the horse to work without getting too hot – heavy sweating will lead to loss of condition and poor performance. Clipping maintains the coat and skin in a healthy condition because it is more difficult to keep heavy coats clean and it lets you observe skin problems. Clipped horses can be groomed more efficiently and can be groomed and rugged up much quicker which prevents them getting chills after working. A final reason is that it improves appearance.

WHEN TO CLIP

Most horses will need clipping from October to January. Depending on the type of horse and the work he is in, it may be necessary to clip as frequently as every two weeks. For horses that are showing in the spring it is best to give the last clip no later than the middle of January to prevent interfering with the new coat coming through. In unusually hot weather or if competing in hot countries it may be necessary to clip during the summer as undue sweating will inhibit performance. This applies particularly to three-day event, show jump and endurance horses, when cooling throughout the competition is one of the most important factors contributing to top performance.

If it is necessary to clip during a three-day event I find that it is better to do so after the dressage phase as clipping the horse may make him fresher and it could affect the performance.

TYPES OF CLIP

Full

Hunter

Blanket

Trace

Chaser　　　　　　　　　*Neck and belly*

Choosing the clip

FULL/HUNTER/HIGH TRACE

Suitable for horses in hard, fast work and or heavy-coated horses to enable them to cool more quickly.

LOW TRACE/BLANKET/CHASER

Horses in lighter work, young horses.

NECK AND BELLY

Horses in light work, ponies, horses that are turned out.

CLIPPING PREPARATIONS

The requirements of the clipping box:
- It must be large enough to enable you to work safely and easily around the horse.
- Good lighting is essential.
- The floor surface must be safe – rubber is ideal, concrete floors should

have some bedding left down to prevent slipping.

- There should be suitable tying-up areas.
- The roof must be high.
- Power points need to be nearby.

Preparing the horse

The horse's coat must be free of mud, sweat and as clean as possible, the less grease in the coat the easier it will be to clip. The clippers will also struggle if the coat is wet so avoid riding before clipping.

The tail can be bandaged or plaited to keep it out of the way. Rugs and blankets should be clean and ready to put on after clipping. If the horse is being clipped for the first time it is an advantage if he has been in a stable next to other horses being clipped – this will familiarize him with the noise of clippers and you will have some idea of how he is likely to react.

EQUIPMENT
- Clippers in good working order
- Sharp blades (preferably two sets)
- Extension lead
- Circuit breaker
- Clipper oil
- Brush and cloth to clean clippers and blades
- Brush for horse
- Something sturdy to stand on
- Chalk/string to help with lines
- Rug to put over horse while clipping
- Skip, shovel and broom

CLIPPING PROCEDURE

It is often advised to give the horse a haynet while clipping but I think this is more of a hindrance as the horse is continuously moving his head and neck which slows the job and it makes it more difficult to get lines straight. If the

An assistant can hold the horse to help keep him relaxed

The clippers should be introduced by placing them on the shoulder

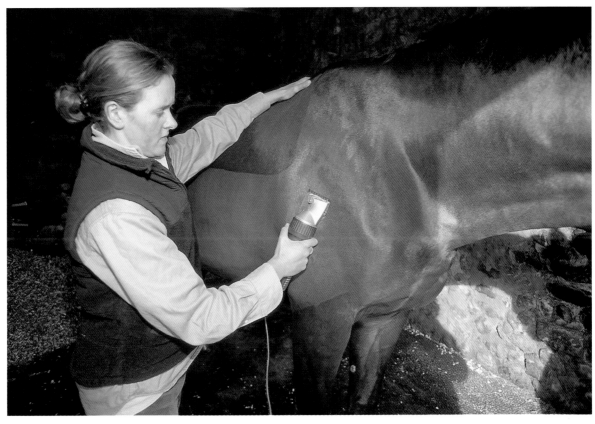

horse has not been clipped before it is advisable to have an assistant to hold him rather than tie him up. This is not always practical in which case I would advise putting the rope through the string but not tying up until the horse is happy and relaxed.

Start by turning the clippers on outside the stable and this will give the horse the chance to become familiar with the noise and you can oil the blades. When the horse looks relaxed with this go into the stable with the clippers turned off, put the clippers onto the horse's shoulder with the blades flat against the coat. Move down the shoulder in the direction of the hair and this will give the horse the feeling of the clippers without the noise and vibration. The shoulder is a good place to start as it is safe, easy to clip and not ticklish. Once the horse has accepted this, stand back and turn the clippers on. If this doesn't disturb him, approach the shoulder, run your hand along the area you intend to clip then repeat as you did with the clippers turned off, running the blades in the direction of the hair. When the horse has adjusted to the feel you can start to clip.

HOW TO CLIP WELL

Clipping well comes with confidence and practise. The first clip you give will probably look a little shabby as the lines may not be straight and often the coat is not clipped close because the blades are not close enough to the skin because of your fear of cutting the horse.

Avoiding 'tram lines'

Tram lines occur when the blades haven't cut against the hair and the clip is not even. When learning to clip always take time to look carefully at how the hair grows before you clip – the coat changes direction in many ways. On the belly and hind quarters it is possible to take long strokes with the clippers and this makes it neater. Always go over a second time as it is likely that hair will be missed due to the blades not being kept flat. In more difficult areas such as the neck it is easier to do shorter strokes and change direction more often; if an area hasn't clipped well try the blades at a different angle and it will clip closer.

Perfecting lines

Decide on the type of clip before you start; if it is a trace or a blanket clip the lines can be drawn on with chalk (unless of course the horse is grey) and this will give you a guide to follow. Clip the easy areas first from both sides and leave perfecting the lines until last, often hours can be spent perfecting one side and then you clip the other side higher and the first side has to be done again. Always make the line lower than you intend it to be as it will get higher as you tidy the clip. Another method is to clip the first side, again not perfecting the lines, start the second side from the hind quarters where you can see both sides to get them level but make sure the horse isn't resting a hind leg. To give a guide down the sides of the horse use a piece of string to measure certain points along the clip; once the basic lines are done both sides can be tidied.

String can be used to make lines more even

Clipping the head

Especial care should be taken when clipping the head and the horse should always be untied and often an assistant is required. For horses that are difficult

I advise investing in a set of small clippers or opting to clip half the head which can look neat if well done. By this I mean that the clip would follow a line from the corners of the horse's mouth, up the face and finish behind the ear. When tacked up this follows the line of the cheek pieces and can be quite well hidden.

Clipping legs

It is very difficult to clip in between the front legs and under the elbows without an assistant. Ideally the legs should be pulled forward, extreme care should be taken as the skin is very loose in this area and it is very easily cut. With some horses it is necessary to clip the legs, for heavy feathered horses the hair can be taken from the back of the legs from the heels to the top of the leg. For a smarter look the legs need to be clipped out, care should be taken around the tendons and when clipping the hindlegs. I suggest that this is not attempted until your horse is one hundred per cent confident with the clippers.

The front leg is pulled forward to clip between the front

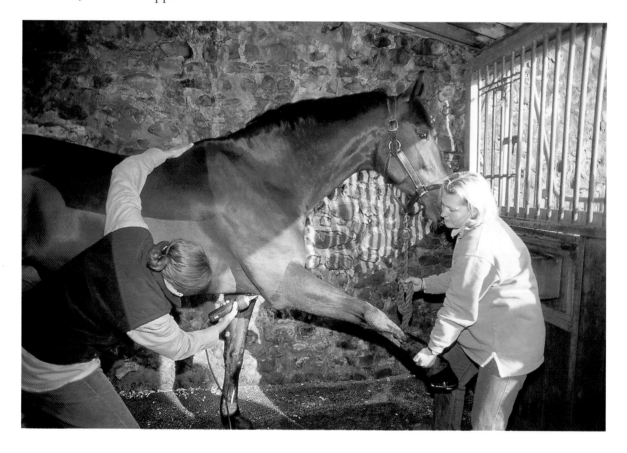

Care after clipping

The horse will have a lot of loose hair and probably very greasy skin if a heavy coat has been removed. Bathing or hot clothing will clean the skin and prevent the horse from itching. Suitable rugs should then be applied to prevent the horse getting cold.

Dealing with difficult horses

For a number of reasons horses can be difficult to clip and these include fear, having a ticklish or sensitive skin, and having had a bad experience being clipped in the past. Clipping a difficult horse can become dangerous and the most important factors to consider are safety to horse and groom.

Assess why the horse is objecting to the clippers; he may be fine in some areas but object to the head or belly and some horses won't tolerate it at all. Certain methods of restraint can be applied for different cases and it is most important not to rush or lose your temper as it will be worse next time. If the horse has a good experience things may improve in the future.

An assistant can hold the horse and reassure him. The assistant must always stand on the same side as you are clipping. If the horse is likely to kick when working around the hind quarters or under the belly the assistant can pick up a front leg. Again, this should be on the same side as you are working.

If the horse will tolerate the twitch and it has the desired effect it is useful for finishing off the difficult areas. The twitch should not be left on for more than twenty minutes therefore this method is not suitable to use for the full duration of clipping.

In some cases the only solution is to have the vet sedate the horse and this is much safer for horse and groom. It is important that all equipment is ready and in good working order, someone experienced will need to clip as the sedation will only last for about forty-five minutes. Most horses tend to sweat when sedated, I tend to clip the head, neck, under the belly and around the hindlegs which is where they are most likely to be difficult and sweat most. A horse under sedation should never be trusted as they often kick out suddenly and unlike with a horse that is fully awake you will not be expecting it.

During the competition season careful planning must be made if the horse is going to need sedation as the withdrawal period is ten days.

CARE OF CLIPPERS AND BLADES

During clipping

Always read instructions carefully on how to use and care for your clippers. The blades must be well oiled before, during and after clipping to prevent damage and heating up. During clipping frequently touch the blades to check how hot they are. If they are too hot to touch they must be allowed to cool down. Hair should be removed frequently from the blades and the air vents of the clippers. I advise removing the blades and thoroughly cleaning several times throughout the clip – failure to do this will lead to damaged clippers or burning the horse.

After clipping

The blades should be removed, all the hair removed and the blades oiled and wrapped in tissue or paper to prevent damage. Store them in a box. The clippers should be thoroughly cleaned and safely stored.

Clipper service

It will depend on how often the clippers are used as to how often they are serviced. All clippers should be done at least once a year and if used frequently then twice a year.

Blade sharpening

Blades should be sharpened after about six heavy clips, less often if clipping lighter coats. Blunt blades can be recognized by the feel and of course if they are not cutting close or are chewing the hair. If you have more than one set of blades they should be labelled to keep track of how often they are used.

CLIPPING RECORDS

Keeping records will help you keep track of how often the blades are used and how good or bad horses are to clip.

EXAMPLE

Horse's name

Date clipped

Type of clip

Name of person who clipped

Blades/clippers used

Comments on how horse behaved

CHAPTER 5
Feeding

Choosing a suitable diet for your horse is important, whether he is used for pleasure or top competition. Studies on the digestive system and equine nutrition have helped us understand the best ways to feed our horses, in order to avoid disorders and produce top performance. Reading up on modern research broadens our knowledge, but the real art of feeding comes from practical experience and knowing your horse well.

The diet of a performance horse is obviously going to differ from that of a pleasure horse. Increased work load requires more energy and stamina. It will also lead to wear and tear, extra nutrients are needed to rebuild and repair body tissues. It is essential to have the horse carrying the correct amount of condition for the job he is doing. Temperament must also be taken into consideration; often we achieve the desired look but find the horse impossible to train. Achieving the correct balance is not always straightforward but can mean the difference between winning and losing.

BASIC RULES OF FEEDING

Before choosing a diet it is important to have a basic knowledge on the rules of feeding.

Points to consider

Feed according to:

- Body weight
- Age
- Type/Temperament
- Work doing
- Rider suitability
- Time of year

This will be discussed later in more detail.

Well-balanced diet

- The diet should contain the essential nutrients in the correct amounts for the work doing.

ESSENTIAL NUTRIENTS

WATER – Will be discussed later.

FIBRE – Essential to ensure the digestive system functions correctly. At least 30% of the diet should be in the form of roughage. The more fibre fed, the less likely the horse is to suffer from digestive disorders.

PROTEIN – Essential for growth and repair to all body tissues.

CARBOHYDRATE – Provides the main source of energy.

FATS AND OILS – Improve skin and coat condition. Provide energy.

VITAMINS AND MINERALS – Essential to balance the diet and ensure the horse is receiving all the nutritional requirements.

Feed little and often

The horse's digestive system is not designed to digest large quantities of food at any one time. In his natural environment, the horse is a 'trickle feeder', consuming relatively small amounts of food at regular intervals. It would not be usual for him to rest for more than three hours before eating again. Therefore feeding twice a day is very unnatural for the horse. Feeding large amounts of concentrates will cause food to be pushed out of the stomach into the small intestine before digestion is complete. Subsequently, the horse will not gain all the nutrients from the food. It may also lead to colic. Avoid feeding more than 2.2kg (5lb) of concentrate feed at any time. Divide the daily concentrate ration into as many small feeds as practical.

Make any changes of feed gradual

The bacteria that aid digestion are specific to each feed stuff. They do not cope well with sudden changes of diet and cause digestive disorders. Introduce new feed by adding 45g (1lb) daily. Colic or change in droppings may suggest the system is not adapting well to the change.

Water should be available at all times

If water is freely available it is not normal for the horse to drink large amounts at any one time, other than after exercise. When the horse has been deprived of water for a long period, for example after travelling, it is important he is allowed to drink before being fed.

Do not feed immediately before hard work

Blood is required for both digestion and exercise. If the horse is made to do strenuous exercise immediately after consuming a large amount of food, digestion can be disrupted. A full stomach can also restrict the expansion of the lungs, therefore sufficient time must be allowed for the stomach to empty before strenuous exercise. Timing of feeding at competitions will be discussed later.

Feed good quality feed

Poor quality feed will lack the essential nutrients, causing loss in condition and poor performance. It will then be necessary to feed more and add supplements to ensure the essential vitamins and minerals are being given. This is a false economy and will work out more expensive than buying a reputable brand of feed. Poor quality roughage will cause respiratory disorders and most certainly inhibit performance. When competing in affiliated competitions, all horses are subject to 'dope testing'. It is recommended to buy feed that is guaranteed to be free of illegal substances.

Keep feeding utensils clean

Always check the feed manger before adding more feed. Any feed left over should be noted and removed before the next feed is given. Buckets and mangers should be scrubbed daily. Automatic water bowls should be checked daily and cleaned at least twice a week.

When adding medication to feed such as Bute or antibiotics, it is recommended that this is put directly into the manger of the intended horse. If it is mixed in a bucket or feed scoop, there is a danger that another horse may be fed from this. It would be a potential problem if the horse were due to compete and be subject to dope testing.

Always use clear and accurate feeding instructions

Feed charts must be kept updated, be clear and easy to follow. All concentrates and roughage should be fed by weight, not volume. Feed scoops should be clearly marked, showing weights, to make feeding more efficient. All feed stuffs weigh differently. For example, 1kg (2lb) of nuts is not the same in volume as 1kg (2lb) of oats. When feeding a variety of feeds, separate feed scoops should be marked for each. Soaked feed stuffs or hay must always be weighed dry.

CHOOSING A SUITABLE DIET

When compiling a diet, we must first estimate the quantity of feed required, then decide on the most suitable types of feed. The following should be considered.

Weight

Use a weigh bridge if possible, if not a weigh tape to estimate your horse's body weight.

The horse should receive 2–2.5% of body weight as his total daily ration. Feeding 2.5% of body weight is suitable for horses in very hard training or to gain condition. 2% of body weight maintains condition and is suitable for horses in moderate work. Feeding less than this will reduce condition.

EXAMPLE

500kg horse – $\dfrac{500}{100}$ = 5 x 2.5 = 12.5kg feed/daily

1100lb horse – $\dfrac{1100}{100}$ = 11 x 2.5 = 27.5lb feed daily

Type

The type or breed of your horse may have an influence on the amount and type of food you give. Typically the thoroughbred tends to be more difficult to keep condition on. The heavier types are more prone to becoming too fat.

Temperament

The type of food we give can have an effect on the horse's temperament. This is a common problem when feeding the competition horse. We must aim to provide the nutrients needed for harder training without causing the horse to become too fresh and difficult to ride.

Age

The young horse, whilst still growing, requires more food than the mature horse. The older horse is often more prone to losing condition and may require a special diet.

Time of year

The diet may change depending on the weather and time of year. During winter months the horse is prone to losing weight due to the fact he is using fat reserves to keep warm. This will be more so with the horse that is living out, however some horses will drop condition even when well rugged and receiving the best care.

The amount of time in the field the horse gets will affect the diet; this will also vary at different times of the year. During spring and early summer, when the grass is very nutritious, horses will quickly gain weight. This must be monitored closely in the competition horse, grazing often has to be restricted to as little as one hour per day.

Rider capability

This has to be taken into consideration. The horse intended for the novice rider must not be fed high energy feeds as it could prove to be unsafe.

Work doing

The diet must suit the individual work programme. Having estimated a required quantity, you must then decide the percentage of roughage to the percentage of concentrates. The following can be used as a guide on which to base the diet; however this will not suit every horse. Condition, temperament, health and performance must be monitored and changes made when necessary.

LEVEL OF WORK	% ROUGHAGE	% CONCENTRATES
Maintenance diet	100	0
Light	80 – 90	10 – 20
Light – Medium	70 – 80	20 – 30
Medium	50 – 60	40 – 50
Medium – Hard	40 – 50	50 – 60
Hard	30 – 40	60 - 70

The minimum amount of roughage should be 30%

MAINTENANCE	Resting or doing very light work. A healthy mature horse will do very well on good quality roughage only, providing sufficient nutrients for hacking and light schooling.
LIGHT WORK	Hacking 1 hour/ day First 4 to 6 weeks of fittening Light schooling Novice dressage and show jump competitions

LIGHT – MEDIUM WORK	1-2 hours Fittening work Novice – Medium dressage Novice – Foxhunter show jumping Pre Novice – Novice event
MEDIUM WORK	Hunting Advanced dressage A & B Show jumper Intermediate eventer 25 to 30 miles Endurance One star three-day eventer
MEDIUM – HARD WORK	Advanced eventer Hunting twice weekly Two star three-day eventer Top level/International show jumper 50 to 75 miles Endurance
HARD WORK	Racing Three and four star three-day eventer 100 mile Endurance

SELECTING APPROPRIATE FEED STUFFS

Having worked out the total amount of feed required and the percentage of roughage to concentrate, the next step is to decide on the most suitable type of feed for your horse.

WHAT THE PERFORMANCE HORSE REQUIRES

Water
(Discussed later)

Fibre

As discussed previously, the digestive system relies on fibre to keep it in good working order. The less fibre the diet contains, the more likely the horse is to suffer from digestive related disorders. More so if the diet is largely made up of cereal type feeds which are high in starch. This can often be recognized by sloppy droppings, containing undigested feed stuffs such as oats.

Fibre can also provide a good source of controlled energy. Digestion takes place in the hind gut where fibre is broken down by the micro organisms. This is converted into energy and can be used immediately or stored in the form of glycogen or fat to be utilized later. The energy provided is slow release, rather than an instant 'buzz', therefore it is less likely to make the horse 'fizzy'. This makes it an ideal diet for the hunter, endurance and event horse.

Fibre also helps to retain water as it moves through the intestinal tract, acting as a fluid and electrolyte reservoir. This can help replace fluids lost through sweating during exercise and competition. Endurance and three-day event horses benefit greatly from this.

Feeding the stabled horse large amounts of roughage will also help to prevent boredom. As discussed previously, the horse has been conditioned to spend a great deal of his time foraging and eating, this gives him a great desire to chew. If deprived of this for long periods of time, problems are likely to arise. It has been proven that horses bedded on straw are less likely to develop stable vices.

Protein

Protein is required for growth and repair. Growing horses and lactating mares require up to 16% protein. Once a horse is fully mature, he will require 8 to 10%. Racehorses are often fed more as they are often working hard as well as maturing physically.

Proteins are made up from amino acids, the three most essential to the horse being lysine, methionine and tryptophan. Grain feeds are typically low in these. Peas, beans, soya-bean meal and lucerne are high.

Complete feeds contain the correct amount of protein essential for the type of work they are intended for. For this reason I would recommend this type of feeding for the performance horse, to ensure he is receiving the correct amounts.

Energy

The harder a horse is training, the more energy he will require. It is important that we feed for the correct type of energy required for specific types of performance. The sprinter requires a short, explosive type of energy. The hunter and endurance horse needs slow release energy to keep him 'fuelled' for a long period of time. The event horse is often the most difficult to balance as he needs to be calm and relaxed for the dressage phase, then ready to jump and gallop for the cross-country. Energy can be derived from the digestion of fibre, starch, oil and protein.

Fibre

As previously discussed, fibre provides slow release energy, ideal for most performance horses.

Starch

Provides a rapid form of energy. Suitable for horses working hard for short periods of time. Very few performance horses benefit from this type of diet as it has a 'heating' effect, making the horse difficult to train. Cereal feeds are typically high in starch – oats 50%, barley 60% and maize 70%.

The digestive system is not designed to cope with large amounts of cereal feed. Starch is digested in the small intestine, which only makes up for about 20% of the gut capacity. Therefore if a big feed is given, consisting largely of cereals, it cannot cope with the quantity of food. Undigested food is then passed on into the large intestine. Here, the fibre digesting bacteria cannot adapt to starch and are often killed off, resulting in disruption to the system. Small invasions may not cause more of a problem than loose droppings but a large invasion may result in laminitis, colic or azoturia.

Most competition horses perform better on a low starch diet, receiving energy from alternative dietry components.

Oil

Provides an alternative source of slow release energy. It is highly digestible and provides up to 2.5 times the energy as feeding an equal amount of grain. Oil is utilized during aerobic exercise only (usually with a heart rate of less than 150). This reduces the use of stored glucose in the muscles, saving it for more intense work or anaerobic activity. By doing this it helps delay the onset of fatigue, which will improve performance. It has also been found to lessen the decline in blood glucose and accelerate the recovery of heart and respiration during the first ten minutes of rest. In practice this has made oil become an increasingly popular form of energy for the endurance and three-day event horse.

There are a variety of oils available. Corn oil has proved to be the most palatable. As with any feed, it must be introduced gradually, starting with only a splash. Often the horse does not like the taste to start and may reject the feed. Chaff in the feed helps to mix it in; adding molasses may disguise the taste. Once the horse is happy with this it can be increased daily, but only by a small amount, so as not to put the horse off. Feeding 80ml (2.7fl oz) per day will improve condition of the coat. More must be fed to provide energy. Horses working very hard such as advanced event horses can be fed up to 450ml (15fl oz) per day. This must be divided into at least two feeds; otherwise the horse is likely not to eat it. When working towards a big competition, the oil must be added to the diet well in advance. For example, if I have a horse aiming for Badminton, at the beginning of May. I will introduce up to 80ml (2.7 fl oz) per day during January. In February I will increase to 200ml (6.7fl oz) per day. The horse will start competing in March and I will increase from 200ml to 400ml (6.7 to 13.4fl oz) by the end of the month. From then on until after Badminton I will feed 400 to 450ml (13.4 to 15.2fl oz) daily. I have found, from personal experience, a great difference in condition and performance from feeding oil.

High oil diets must be supplemented with vitamin E and selenium, this will be discussed in 'supplements'.

Protein

Can provide energy but is not a good source. Increased protein should not be fed to increase energy. Feeding large amounts will also increase the water requirements of the horse; this may effect performance and result in dehydration.

Vitamins and minerals

All horses require vitamins and minerals if they are to remain healthy. The horse which is feeding on good grass or a well balanced diet should be receiving the necessary requirements. Feeding a suitable, reputable compound feed can almost guarantee this. Traditional feeding is not so reliable and it would be advisable to seek advice on feeding a broad spectrum vitamin and mineral supplement.

The performance horse often takes much more out of himself during training, travelling and competition. For this reason it is sometimes necessary to supplement the diet with extra vitamins and minerals. Knowing exactly what is required can be difficult, health, condition and performance are good indicators, but the signs often come too late. Once your horse has reached medium level work, it is advisable to seek advice from a nutritionist, to ensure you are feeding the essential requirements. Most reputable feed companies have a help line. (Supplements will be discussed later.)

TRADITIONAL FEEDING

I am not totally opposed to traditional feeding as I have known of horses fed this way to produce top results. What we must not forget is that feeding a top performance horse requires more skill and precision than feeding the pleasure horse. Therefore, I would advise this method of feeding to be practised only by knowledgeable and experienced grooms and stable managers.

COMPOUND FEEDS

A compound feed, such as a cube or mix is a ready made balanced diet. It contains a variety of feed stuffs with added vitamins and minerals to suit individual requirements ranging from 'Horse and Pony Cubes' to 'Racehorse Cubes'. This is the simplest and most reliable way of ensuring that your horse receives the correct nutrients required for a healthy life. The traditional method of feeding is not so reliable and requires more skill and experience.

I have always found it possible to select a compound feed to suit each individual. By doing this, the diet is based on what is scientifically correct for that horse. It is then important to monitor health, condition and performance, and make necessary changes. This may be by adjusting the amounts or altering the type of cube or mix. It may also require adding to the feed; in theory some would say this is unbalancing the diet. This may be true but if it has the desired effect, it cannot be wrong. The skill of feeding comes from experimenting and not being afraid to make changes to suit the individual. The most important aspect is to recognize early, the mental and physical signs, showing a particular diet does not suit. From this experience the art of feeding will be mastered.

ROUGHAGE

We must also consider the type of roughage that will best suit our horse. Whatever choice is made, the nutritional value and cleanliness of the forage is of utmost importance to the performance horse.

Hay

Hay is the most commonly fed source of roughage in this country. It is important that the hay is of good quality, in order to provide the nutrients and eliminate the risk of causing respiratory disorders. Making hay at the right time is necessary to preserve the nutrients. Hay that is rained on during making and baled when still wet will be of poor quality and cause the most problems.

Competition horses, that are expected to jump and gallop must be free from the risk of all respiratory disorders, if they are to perform well. Feeding poor quality hay will certainly predispose them to problems.

QUALITIES OF GOOD HAY
- Smells sweet
- Not too pale in colour
- Free from dust when shaken
- Free from mould
- Contains a variety of good grasses
- Free from weeds

The only way to ensure the hay is good quality is to have it analyzed. This is only practical when buying in bulk. Otherwise it is advisable to buy from a reputable stockist.

MEADOW HAY

This is made from a permanent pasture. Good quality will contain a variety of grasses, providing good nutritional value. More so than seed hay as it is less fibrous.

SEED HAY

Made from grass that has been specifically grown for hay. The pasture will be sown and ploughed within five years. It produces much more fibrous, coarser hay. Seed hay is usually of good quality as more care is taken when making. This does however make it more expensive to buy.

SOAKING HAY

All hay contains mould spores, and poor quality obviously has many more than good quality hay. When inhaled, these spores may irritate the airways, causing respiratory disorders. Some horses will not be affected by a mild invasion; others are allergic to the smallest amount. Soaking hay helps to prevent the spores entering the airways; instead they are chewed and swallowed, causing no harm to the lungs.

The correct quantity of hay must be weighed before soaking. It must then be totally immersed in water for 10 to 20 minutes, any longer than this causes the nutrients to be lost. It should then be drained and fed.

This can be very time consuming when feeding a large number of horses. It is also not practical to feed during travel and competition. For these reasons, haylage is becoming an increasingly popular choice for feeding the competition horse.

Haylage

Haylage is made from grass that is cut, baled and sealed in airtight bags or wrapping. This reduces the amount of dust and fungal spores. When using home grown haylage, it is necessary to have it analyzed for nutritional value and PH level and this will ensure it is safe to feed and give you an idea of the quality. It is often higher in nutrients than hay, therefore less concentrates are required.

Haylage has higher water content than hay, it is necessary to feed more in weight to ensure the horse is receiving sufficient fibre.

Buying big bales can prove economical for a large yard. This is not a suitable option for a small yard or one horse owner. The bale must be used up within two to three days of opening. It is possible to buy in smaller bales to suit one horse or to use when travelling and competing. This does however work out quite expensive.

Care must be taken when storing or moving the bales not to puncture the plastic wrap as this will allow air to enter making it unsafe for the horse to eat.

Feeding hay/haylage

Hay or haylage can be fed from the ground or in a haynet or rack. Feeding from the ground is my preference as it is the most natural way for the horse to eat. It is also better for the horse with a respiratory disorder to have the head lowered, rather than carrying it high. If the horse is very wasteful and tends to trample the food around the bed, it may help to feed smaller quantities more frequently. If this is not practical it may be necessary to use the net or rack. This method may also help to alleviate boredom if the horse eats very quickly. When using a haynet it is important that it is not left hanging low in the stable when empty, especially overnight. I have known of horses to roll and get a food stuck, causing panic and considerable injury.

WATER

Water is the most essential of all nutrients. Without water the horse would not survive for more than six days, he could however last for two to three weeks without food. Deprived of water, the horse will quickly become dehydrated, affecting performance and resulting in serious problems.

Water not only prevents dehydration, but aids a number of bodily functions: the digestive system, the circulatory system, the regulation of body temperature and it provides a basis for tears, mucus, joint oil and milk. An adult, healthy horse will drink between 23 and 68 litres (5 and 15 gallons) of water per day. This will be considerably increased during hot weather. Whenever possible the horse should have a constant supply of clean fresh water available at all times. In the stable this can be administered in buckets or automatic drinkers.

Buckets

The main advantage of using buckets is to monitor drinking. This is particularly important when the horse is sick, or if you suspect your horse may not be drinking sufficient amounts and this is very important when the horse is in hard training. If ever in any doubt, buckets must be used. The disadvantages of using buckets are that they are time consuming, get kicked over and broken, fill up with bedding and the horse may be left without water.

If possible it is safer to have the buckets hung in the stable rather than on the floor. Always check water after feeding and exercise as this is when the horse is most likely to drink.

Automatic drinkers

The advantages of these are that they are much more practical on a large yard and they ensure the horse has water at all times.

The disadvantages however are that drinking cannot be monitored. If you suspect the horse is not drinking, the drinker must be covered and buckets provided as an alternative. In cold weather they may freeze, the horse may roll and injure himself or cause damage to the drinker, resulting in a very wet bed.

Drinkers must be checked twice a day and cleaned at least every other day. Certain types can be difficult to clean.

Dehydration

The horse can become dehydrated from a lack of water or due to fluids being lost quicker than they are replaced.

CAUSES

- Deprived of water.
- Refusing to drink. This is commonly caused by stress, often during travel or competition.
- During cold weather the horse will often drink less than he requires. Cold icy water will often put them off. This is frequently made worse by the fact we often feed more roughage during cold weather, which requires a large volume of water for digestion.
- Excessive sweating during training, competition, travelling, stress or hot weather.
- Illness including diarrhoea (more common in foals), excessive urination, and haemorrhage.

SYMPTOMS

The most common indicator of dehydration is to pinch a fold of skin from the neck or point of shoulder, when released it should return to normal immediately. If it remains folded or is slow to return, the horse is quite seriously dehydrated. Other symptoms include:

- Dry mouth.
- Mucous membranes pale.
- Slow heart rate recovery.
- Poor performance/reduced stamina.
- Tucked up.
- Eyes sunken.
- Loss of appetite.
- Reluctance to drink. Mild dehydration will stimulate thirst. If water is not offered the condition worsens, the desire to drink will then become less and less and the horse will refuse to drink. At this stage the vet will be required to administer fluids intravenously or through a stomach tube.

As little as 2 to 3% dehydration will affect performance. Unfortunately, this is often not recognized as being the cause and the horse may be punished for going badly; 7 to 10% dehydration will have a more serious affect on health and may result in:

- Colic
- Laminitis

A fold of skin can be taken from the neck or point of shoulder to check for dehydration

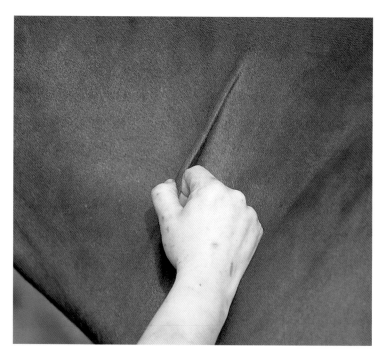

- Azoturia
- Muscle Damage
- Poor performance, resulting in a fall or serious leg injury
- Thumps (synchronous diaphragmatic flutter)
- Dehydration of 15 to 20% can cause death

ALL OF THE ABOVE ARE SERIOUS CONDITIONS AND WILL NEED IMMEDIATE VETERINARY ATTENTION

In taking care of the horse, whenever possible, we must prevent the horse reaching the above stages of dehydration, at home, during travel or competition.

PREVENTION

- Whenever possible provide free access to fresh clean water.
- When not possible, for example during travel or competition, the horse must be offered water at least every half hour. More frequently after exercise until thirst is quenched.
- Ensure the horse is fit enough for the job he is doing. The fitter a horse is the less demand is put on the body, therefore he will sweat less.
- Ensure the horse is well hydrated before a long journey or competition, especially in hot weather. It may be necessary to seek veterinary advice if your horse is reluctant to drink. They may suggest administering fluids intravenously or through a stomach tube prior to departure or competition.
- Always use buckets to monitor drinking during illness, competition or hard periods of training.
- Add 1 to 2 tablespoons of salt to the diet daily, depending on weather conditions and level of training.
- Some horses are fussy about drinking strange water when away from home. Flavouring the water may encourage drinking. Experiment at home prior to the competition, until you find a taste your horse likes. The following have been known to work: sugar, glucose, cider vinegar, apple juice, molasses.
- An alternative option is to carry water from home in containers but this is only practical for short trips.

- Feed electrolytes to horses in medium to hard work, during travel and competition.

Electrolytes

Electrolytes are the essential minerals or body salts present in the body. Their role is to maintain fluid balance within cells. The most important electrolytes are sodium, potassium, chloride, calcium and magnesium. They are continuously lost from the body, primarily through sweat. This can often be recognized by the thick foamy consistency. The more conditioned a horse, the thinner the sweat becomes.

WATER ALONE WILL NOT REPLACE ELECTROLYTES

WHEN TO FEED
- All horses in medium and above work.
- Travelling long distances (four hours or more).
- When competing.
- During hot weather.
- Following certain illness (take veterinary advice).
- Should be introduced before they are required to ensure the horse will eat or drink them.

HOW TO FEED
Fresh clean water must be available at all times. Feeding electrolytes without water can worsen a problem

IN THE WATER
Liquid or powder can be added to the water. It is important to provide two buckets, one containing electrolytes, the other without. It has been said if the body needs electrolytes they will taste sweet and the horse will want to drink. If they don't need them, the taste is offensive. I have had experience of horses that have drunk electrolytes in preference to fresh water for a period of time and then changed to the fresh water and no longer wanted to drink the electrolytes. This would support the theory. I have had other horses' that have shown no interest in drinking

electrolytes, even after serious competing and travelling. Another disadvantage is the powder often settles on the bottom of the bucket and the horse doesn't receive any of it.

IN THE FEED

Liquids and powders can be added to the feed. It mixes in better with chaff or sugar beet. This is a more reliable way of feeding, and would be my choice. It is however very important to ensure the horse is drinking well.

SYRINGE

A paste can be administered by syringe. This is a more popular choice for endurance riders during competition. Again it is essential that the horse is drinking well.

PRE COMPETITION

During competition, electrolytes should not be given too close to exercise. It is advisable to give the night before as it can take up to six hours for the horse to drink enough to become fully hydrated again.

POST COMPETITION

The sooner fluids and electrolytes are replaced after strenuous exercise, the quicker the horse will recover. This is highly important during a three-day event or a show taking place over a several days. The same would apply after travelling a long distance to a competition, or when having to travel a long distance after competition. I had an experience of a horse becoming seriously dehydrated travelling back to England from a competition in Germany. He had competed in a three-day event in quite hot weather conditions. Due to another horse being injured, which we were travelling with, we had to leave immediately after the prize giving, not giving my horse a chance to relax and drink before loading. Considering the level of competition and weather conditions, it is highly likely that he was mildly dehydrated before departure. He then refused to drink for the eighteen hour journey. On arrival at home I had a seriously dehydrated horse, requiring immediate veterinary attention. Luckily he made a full recovery. This taught me a great lesson. I now insist my horses are given sufficient time to relax and recover after competition, before travelling a long distance. I monitor their drinking very closely and if ever in doubt I would always seek veterinary advice before departure.

There are many electrolytes available on the market. Ensure you select a brand containing the essential minerals. Added carbohydrate will aid absorption and glucose gives a more favourable taste. During the competition season, it is advisable to seek advice from a nutritionist on a suitable brand for your horse. Always ensure the product is guaranteed against prohibited substances.

SUPPLEMENTS

Feeding a supplement means you are adding to the diet something that it is lacking. A healthy horse, in medium work or lower, receiving a suitable balanced diet should not require supplements, other than a tablespoon of salt daily. Compound feeds contain the correct vitamin and mineral balance for the level of work for which they are intended. This, accompanied by good quality roughage, in most cases ensures the nutritional requirements for the performance horse are met.

When to feed supplements
- Traditional feeding methods are not as reliable as compound feeds. Cereal feeds are often low in essential vitamins and minerals. Feeding a broad spectrum multi vitamin and mineral supplement will top up the deficiencies.
- During hard training and competition. Horses performing at top level may require extra vitamins and minerals. The most common of these is electrolytes, as previously discussed. Vitamin E and selenium may also be required. When feeding a horse at this level it is advisable to discuss the diet with a nutritionist.
- Travelling which often causes stress and dehydration.
- Following ill health.
- When feeding a high oil diet.

Most common supplements fed to the performance horse

BROAD SPECTRUM MULTI-VITAMIN AND MINERAL

WHEN TO USE
- The diet does not reach the nutritional requirements.
- Horses on a low concentrate diet. This could be due to temperament, condition, ill health or injury.
- Supplement cereal diets.
- Fussy eaters who often don't finish their food.
- Horses performing at top level in medium – hard work.

VITAMIN E AND SELENIUM
Supports muscle function and immunity.

WHEN TO USE
- During hard training.
- When feeding a high oil diet.

Extra stress and injury placed on top performance horses will result in a 'free radical' attack (molecules formed as a result of normal body processes). These are dangerous chemicals that cause internal cell damage. This can result in poor performance, ill health and lameness. Feeding a high oil diet will also increase the production of 'free radicals'. Antioxidants are the body's natural defence against free radical attack. By catching and neutralizing the free radicals, they prevent damage to cells.

Vitamin E and selenium, along with vitamins A and C are the most powerful antioxidants in the diet.

PROBIOTICS
Probiotic are live micro-flora (good bug) supplements that help restore the correct balance of micro-flora in the gut. This is essential in preventing digestive disorders and to ensure optimum nutrient intake, vitamin production and boosting the immune system.

The competition horse is frequently subjected to stress during hard training, travelling, competing, change of routine and injury. This can often have a serious negative impact on the digestive system, resulting in diarrhoea or colic. Feeding a dietry probiotic helps to repopulate the micro-flora present in the gut, preventing digestive disorders and ensuring maximum use of food given.

WHEN TO USE

- During hard training and competition.
- Travelling long distances or to bad travellers.
- Horses that become stressed during competition.
- Following digestive disorders.
- Following worming or antibiotic treatment.

Probiotics are available as a specific supplement or as part of a feed balancer. In my experience I have found a feed balancer to be sufficient under normal circumstances. I tend to feed a specific probiotic supplement during long periods of travel, top level competition or following digestive disorders.

PREBIOTICS

As previously discussed the food digesting bacteria present in the gut adapt to cope with the feed stuffs they are being fed. Changes in the diet must be gradual to allow the bacteria to adjust, otherwise diarrhoea and colic can result. Supplementing a prebiotic will feed the bacteria in the gut, stimulating the growth of numbers. This ensures the population remains high throughout the dietry changeover.

Other than reducing the risk of digestive disorders, feeding a prebiotic will ensure better feed utilization and may reduce behavioural problems caused by dietry changes.

WHEN TO USE

- During periods of dietry changes at home, during travel or competition.
- During changes in feeding routines.
- When bringing horses in from grass and introducing concentrates to the diet.

JOINT SUPPLEMENTS

Feeding a joint supplement to the performance horse has become increasingly popular. The aim is to combat general wear and tear on the joints. This is more crucial for horses in hard training or as they become older. Joint supplements do this in several ways:

- Help in the formation of synovial fluid, responsible for lubricating the joint.
- Aid in production of cartilage which is essential for optimum joint function.
- Reduce inflammation.

WHAT THEY CONTAIN

- Glucosamine and chrondroitin are the most common ingredients which are responsible for the formation of synovial fluid and production of cartilage.
- Manganese which also aids in the production of cartilage.
- MSM (methyl-sulphonyl-methane) which has anti-inflammatory properties which aid muscle recovery and promote circulation. MSM has been shown to complement the action of glucosamine. It also has antioxidant properties, helping to combat the attack of free radicals.
- Devil's claw which is a natural herb which acts as an anti-inflammatory.

There are many joint supplements available to choose from. Some contain other vitamins, minerals and herbs. It is not necessary to select a brand containing the most ingredients. If the diet is balanced, other nutrients will already be provided. The most important ingredients are the ones stated above.

WHEN TO FEED

- Horses in hard training.
- Older horses.
- Young horses with 'star potential'.
- Horses with joint problems.

Joint supplements can prove quite costly but they do work. Remember that 'prevention is better than cure'. We must aim to preserve our horses the best we can to enable them to train and compete for a number of years.

CALMERS

In my mind feeding supplementary calmers to the performance horse has to be questioned. Products claim to 'maintain calm temperament', 'avoid stress and behavioural problems', others even state it will mildly sedate the horse, without effecting performance. I do not agree it is possible to mildly sedate without performance being inhibited. We have to consider the affect it may have on performance. In the case of a dressage horse, it may enable the excitable to remain more relaxed and produce a better test. Providing all substances used are prohibited, this is totally acceptable. Show jumping and cross-country must be looked at from a different prospect. If a product is having a calming affect, will the horse jump and gallop as well? And more importantly, when going cross-country, faced with solid obstacles, will the horse react as quickly when in trouble and be able to extract himself out of a difficult situation? I don't believe his reactions would be as sharp.

Calmers are a very popular supplement for the event horse. Producing a calm dressage test out of a horse that is ready to gallop and jump can often be difficult and frustrating. All too often riders turn to calmers as a solution. In my opinion, extreme care should be taken when feeding a calmer to subdue a horse in order to produce a good dressage, then expecting the horse to jump out of the start box, full of enthusiasm for the cross-country, often less than three hours later. I have known very reliable jumping horses to make mistakes on the cross-country when calmers have been given for the dressage. It is in the best interest of horse and rider to put safety first.

WHAT THEY CONTAIN

The most common base for a calmer is magnesium. Having used this I have found it to have very little effect and certainly has not been detrimental to performance. Herbal calmers often contain passion flower, hawthorn, chamomile, vervain and valerian.

When feeding calmers, always ensure it is a guaranteed product that does not contain any prohibited substances. Many will contain valerian which is now banned. Before turning to calmers, consider your horse's diet. Are you feeding for instant energy, which will often make the horse very excitable? If so change the diet to slow release energy. Using a supplement to aid digestion may also improve temperament. When nutrients pass through the gut too quickly, they often go undigested, causing a build up of acid. Slowing down the rate of passage of food through the gut, allows more effective digestion and less acid build up. This often helps maintain calm temperament and may also prevent stable vices.

HERBAL SUPPLEMENTS

Due to the concern regarding long term effects of using conventional drugs and antibiotics, many people now turn to herbal remedies for treatment or preventative measures. Herbs are also becoming an increasingly popular choice for treating the horse. Companies offer a range of products to treat all systems and disorders. The most commonly used on the competition horse being those associated with mobility, respiration and the nervous system. They can be very expensive to buy but do tend to have a positive affect. As with all supplements, it is vital to ensure the product you use is free from prohibited substances.

MONITORING CONDITION

The diet of the competition horse is likely to change fairly frequently. This may be as often as once a week during a fittening programme. Once the horse has reached a desired level of fitness, it is more likely to stabilize.

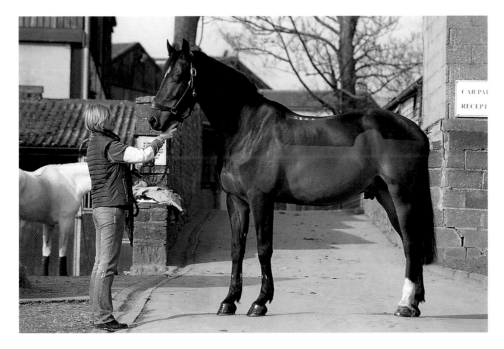

A well-conditioned dressage horse

Monitoring condition is where the real art of feeding comes into play. Designing a diet is pretty straightforward, with the help of a book or advice from a nutritionist. Unfortunately your book cannot tell you when it is going wrong and the diet is not suiting your horse. All too often the early signs are not recognized. People often think their horse has lost weight over night because suddenly he looks thin. This is rarely the case; they have failed to notice the slight changes. Developing an eye comes through years of practice and experience. What we must not forget is that no two horses are ever the same and we must feed and assess each as an individual.

Points to consider are:

- Condition/weight of your horse
- Desired energy level/performance requirements
- Health
- Temperament

Assessing condition is one of the obvious ways of telling us that we are feeding correctly. It is important to have in mind an ideal picture of how you want your horse to look. This will vary depending on the job he has to do. For example, the dressage horse will carry more weight and be rounder in

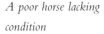

A poor horse lacking condition

appearance than the event horse, which will be more 'streamline'. Type, breed and age must be taken into consideration as they may prevent you from reaching the desired look. With a goal in mind, it is important to have a method of monitoring condition.

Condition scoring

This is a method that anyone can do, but does require a trained eye. If you only have one or two horses it will help to spend time assessing others. A

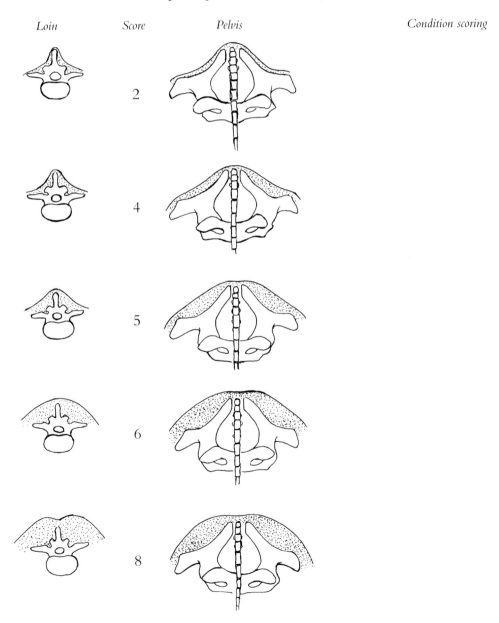

Condition scoring

horse sale is an ideal place to do this. It will give you the opportunity to see all shapes and sizes, fat and thin. A day spent doing this is invaluable. It is also helpful to spend time looking at horses in competition. Compare the condition of horses competing at different levels. Observing horses ridden by professionals should give you a good idea of what you are aiming for.

HOW TO CONDITION SCORE

The horse should have his rugs removed and be standing where he can be viewed from the side and rear. If the horse is cold he may appear tucked up and give a false picture. He may also be bloated if he has been out at grass.

Using a condition scoring chart, compare your horse and decide on his score. The following is on a scale of 1 to10. Other books may show 1 to 5. Your horse should come between 5 and 7. If he is not in this range the diet must be considered.

SCORE 1

Starvation level. Croup (sacral) and hip bones (pelvis) prominent and very sharp, especially over points. A marked hollow in front of the withers. A very deep temporal fossa and possibly a sunken eye. Spinous processes of the vertebrae are well defined. Rib cage prominent with all ribs showing from behind foreleg muscles.

SCORE 2

Ribs easily visible. Contour sunken either side of backbone. Spinous processes well defined. Quarters sunken, pelvis and croup points well defined. Deep depression under and either side of the tail. Bones palpable.

SCORE 3

Withers, croup and backbone processes and points still clearly defined. A little more muscle definition but still hollow in front of the wither. Slight cavity under tail.

SCORE 4

Front half of rib cage covered, back half still visible. Neck beginning to fill up in front of the wither. Spinous processes still palpable.

SCORE 5

Approaching normal for degree of fitness or rest. Withers, croup and hip bones palpable with pressure but some muscle definition developing.

SCORE 6

Normal. Firm, muscled neck. Ribs just covered but palpable. Haunch, croup bone and buttocks covered but easily felt. Muscles well defined.

SCORE 7

Beginning to carry too much weight. Slight crest development. Ribs well covered, requiring firm pressure to palpate. Pelvis and croup well covered.

SCORE 8

Fat. Definition of bones, except at points, lost. A hollow gutter from croup to tail. Neck becoming hard and cresty.

SCORE 9

Obese. Ribs, quarters and back buried in fat. Deep palpation necessary to feel croup and hip bones. Loaded shoulder fat; beginnings of a hollow from wither to croup.

SCORE 10

Very obese. Marked crest. Neck very wide and firm. Deep hollow from wither to tail. Back broad and flat. Huge pads of fat on shoulders and quarters. Pelvis and croup buried. Skin distended. Lumbar region 'raised'.

Time should be taken to condition score at least once a week. During the summer we tend to see our horses without rugs on every day. In winter we often only remove half the rug at a time when grooming and tacking up, not seeing the horse as a whole. This is when we are most likely to miss the early changes in condition.

USING A WEIGH TAPE

A weigh tape can be used to gain a rough estimate of your horse's body weight. This is useful to know and can help in compiling a diet. The tape can be purchased quite cheaply from most tack or feed suppliers. Measuring your

A weigh tape can be used to estimate body weight

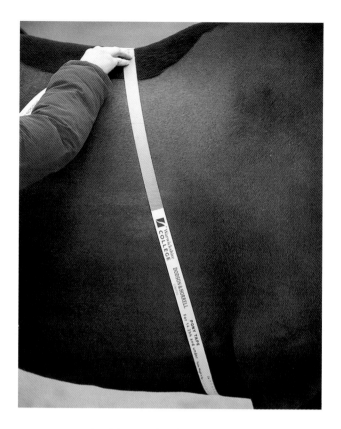

horse weekly will give you a rough idea whether he is maintaining condition. The tape should not be relied upon, it is important that you condition score as well.

USING A WEIGHBRIDGE

Weighing the horse on a weighbridge is the most accurate method of obtaining and maintaining body weight. The majority of professional competition yards use this method.

WHEN TO WEIGH

Routine weighing should happen at least once a week. It is essential to weigh at the same time of day, the most accurate time being first thing in the morning, before feeding. The horse should not be weighed immediately after coming in from the field.It may be necessary to weigh your horse more frequently if he has problems maintaining body weight. Again it is important to condition score and not rely entirely on the reading of the weighbridge.

The weighbridge is also very useful to use during the competition

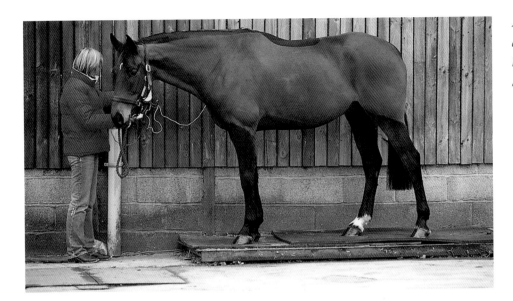

season. Often a horse can go to a competition looking very well and come back looking thin and 'tucked up'. The majority of time this is due to fluid loss. Very few horses drink sufficient amounts during travel and competition. If I have a horse I am particularly worried about, I weigh before leaving for the competition and again when I return home. This must be done immediately before the horse drinks. I have had horses lose up to 30kg (66lb) over two days. The weight should then be taken again the next morning and each day until you are satisfied the horse is fully hydrated.

I condition score and weigh all my horses the morning after a competition. Often a horse will look fitter after a cross-country run. When working towards a three-day event this is usually what you are aiming for. If I feel the horse has lost too much weight, I must consider the diet and work programme for the next week.

All weights should be recorded, along with the date and comments. This is very useful to look back on and use as a guideline.

EXAMPLE:

1 January	Patch	620 – Walk exercise 1 hour/day
		Condition score 7 (looks fat)
1 February	Patch	608 – Hacking 1 to 2 hours/day and schooling
		Condition score 6 to 7
		Top line building up not as much belly

1 March   Patch 596 – Hacking 1 to 2 hours/day, schooling,
                         show jumping
                         Condition score 6. Looks good

1 April   Patch 582 – Ready for one-day event
                         Condition score 6. Quite lean
                         Ribs not seen but easily felt
                         Ideal one-day event weight

10 May   Patch 570 – Ideal three-day event weight
                         Condition score 5 to 6. Very lean. Ribs visible

This system tells me what each horse's weight should be at each level of fitness. Younger horses will change slightly until they are six or seven. This is not as important as they are not competing at a high level.

Developing an eye

Most of us have a picture in our mind of the 'ideal horse' and how we would like our horse to look. This may resemble a top show jumper after watching the Hickstead Derby, or you may have seen the winning horse trotting up in front of Badminton House. What we must remember is to get a horse to that level takes years of training, feeding alone does not achieve this.

Word Perfect, winner of Badminton in 1998, who I have taken care of since he was a five-year-old, was a very late developer. Although he reached international level at the age of eight, in my mind, he didn't look his best until he was twelve. It is important to be patient and realistic about what you want to achieve. Always take into consideration age, type and breed as this may affect performance.

It is a common mistake when trying to get a horse fit to end up with him too thin. An inexperienced person may have a problem recognizing the difference between fit and poor condition. Both will carry very little fat and show ribs.

POOR CONDITION
- Very little fat covering the ribs and spine.

- Neck weak and underdeveloped.
- Hind quarters hollow and sunken.
- Belly may appear distended.
- Coat staring, dull eyes.

FIT
- Ribs visible or easily felt.
- Tummy tight (very fit horses may appear herring gutted).
- Neck and top line well developed.
- Muscles on the shoulders and hind quarters are well defined.
- The horse in general looks healthy, bright eyes, good shine to coat.

DEALING WITH DIFFICULT FEEDERS

Some horses are much easier to feed than others. The competition horse requires essential nutrients, while maintaining a suitable body weight and a reasonable temperament. Finding the right balance can prove difficult.

Fussy eaters
The performance horse is subjected to high levels of stress, due to hard training, travelling and competing. One of the most common symptoms of stress is loss of appetite. This can be a cause for concern in the hard working horse.

The horse may go off his feed for several reasons:
- He dislikes the taste of something new added to the feed.
- The diet has been increased and the horse is faced with too much food.
- There are teeth problems.
- He has a sore mouth.
- He is in poor health.
- He is suffering from stress.

Stress
Before considering stress, rule out other causes for concern. If the horse is not usually fussy and suddenly goes off his feed, he may be ill. His

temperature should be taken immediately. Other problems are usually easily dealt with, stress can be more difficult. It is usually prompted by a hard training session, travel or change in routine.

WHAT TO DO

ENSURE THE HORSE IS DRINKING – Water is much more important than food. If the horse is not drinking he will quickly become dehydrated leading to illness and poor performance. Always use buckets to monitor water intake. Regularly check for signs of dehydration. If your horse is not drinking well over a big competition it is advisable to discuss options with the vet. In my experience stomach tubing on the morning of the cross-country and again after the cross-country has helped. It can certainly do no harm and may avoid a serious problem. This must be done by an official competition veterinary.

ENCOURAGE FIBRE – Fibre is more important than concentrates. Fussy feeders do not tend to lack energy. Reduction in fibre may cause digestive disorders, especially if the diet is high in starch. Try feeding a combination of hay and haylage. Chaff, Alfa A and Readigrass are alternative options.

FEED LITTLE AND OFTEN – If the horse refuses to eat, remove the feed. Try a small amount after exercise. Offer small feeds frequently throughout the day. Feed a larger amount at night. Always remove uneaten food before adding new.

GIVE DIFFERENT TYPES OF FEED – If the horse has refused to eat for a number of days it is worth trying a different feed. You may find something that works.

FEED A BROAD SPECTRUM VITAMIN AND MINERAL SUPPLEMENT – When food intake is lower than recommended it is advisable to add a vitamin and mineral supplement as the horse may be lacking in these. This should be added into the night feed which is most likely to be eaten.

REDUCE WORK LOAD – The horse may benefit from having the pressure taken off him for a couple of days. If he can become more relaxed in himself he may gain his appetite again.

GRASS – The majority of horses will eat grass, although I have known some horses to go out and stand at the gate. If grass is what the horse wants, offer as much as possible. During competition it will be necessary to hand graze frequently.

ADDITIVES – Try adding carrots and apples to the feed. Molasses is very sweet and can be used to tempt or disguise an unpleasant taste.

If nothing works, do not be too alarmed. I have learnt through experience that the horse can live on very little, and will eat when he is hungry. Word Perfect was one of the most difficult horses I have had to feed. I remember the anxiety he caused me at Badminton in 1998. We arrived at the event on Tuesday; he refused to eat anything, other than a small amount of Readigrass until Friday. He still managed to put up a top class performance and win the competition.

Weight loss

CAUSES
- Horse not eating
- Not feeding enough for the work doing
- Cold
- Old age
- Worms
- Teeth problems
- Ill health
- Poor quality feed

The most common causes in the competition horse are not eating enough due to stress or not being fed sufficient for the work load. People often under feed for fear of having the horse too fresh. This can be rectified by changing to an alternative source of energy such as fibre or oil. Oil will also help maintain condition.

Feeding a probiotic or feed balancer can aid digestion and improve condition. Feeds such as showing chaff or high calorie milk pellets are an excellent source of protein and may also work.

If the horse eats well but does not gain weight it is likely he may have a more serious problem and it is advisable to seek veterinary advice.

The fat horse

In my view a performance horse that is too fat is far more at risk than if too thin. Asking an over weight horse to work hard, at any discipline, adds a tremendous amount of physical stress. Obviously the dressage horse and show jumper can carry more weight than an event horse, as it is not expected to gallop. However, top level competition requires hard training and far too often I see horses that are too fat.

FITTENING

It is a mistake to allow the horse to get too fat during periods of rest. The over weight horse takes longer and is much harder to get fit. It adds more strain and increasing wear and tear onto the legs. Long term this will lead to lameness.

CONTROLLING WEIGHT

If the horse is not allowed to become too fat it will be much easier to control his weight. Unfortunately if the horse has gained weight the only way to reduce it is to feed less than the work load requires. Feeding 1.5% body weight daily to a horse in work should reduce body weight. This may result in the horse lacking energy and becoming sour in his temperament. Try to motivate by varying the work programme. Feed little and often to prevent him standing without food for hours. Feeding from a haynet with small holes will make hay last longer. Turning out in a small well grazed paddock will entertain the horse, hopefully without gaining weight.

Try to reduce weight early in the fittening programme when the work is light. As the work load increases the horse will require more nutrients. A common mistake people make is to feed too much, early on. They then panic because the horse is too fat for the competition. Feed is then reduced at a time energy is required.

When feeding this type of horse I do the opposite. In preparing for a three-day event, I aim to have the horse lighter in condition than necessary a month before the event. In the last month the feed is increased to build up the energy supplies. The horse arrives at the event feeling very well and ready to go, not hungry, sour and over worked.

Remember to always add a broad spectrum vitamin and mineral supplement when feeding reduced rations.

FEEDING DURING COMPETITIONS

Water

Whenever possible the horse must have fresh water freely available. During a one-day competition water should be offered:

- On arrival.
- After exercise.
- At least every hour during periods between classes.
- In hot weather, water should be freely available or offered every half hour.
- Never deprive the horse of water before the cross-country.
- Always allow the horse to drink if he goes to the bucket; if he is blowing hard, limit the intake to a few mouthfuls and keep him walking afterwards. I often find the horse wants to drink immediately after the cross-country but once recovered will refuse water.
- If the horse is very thirsty, allow a quarter of a bucket frequently until thirst is quenched.
- Frequently offer water during long periods of travel, especially after competition.
- On arrival home, provide two buckets of water, one containing electrolytes.
- If your stable has a small automatic drinker, always provide buckets as an alternative. Often the horse will empty the drinker and not wait for it to refill. He will then eat. This could be a potential problem if the horse is already dehydrated from competition.
- Water buckets should be checked and refilled as late as possible.

Feeding

TYPES OF FEED

When competing away from home for a period of time it is advisable to take your own feed and hay/haylage. If you intend to travel abroad always check that the country you are going to doesn't hold any restrictions on the importation of feed stuffs. If this is the case, find out what feed is going to be available. This should be introduced to your horse's diet well before departure.

It is more common to change the source of roughage. Small bales of haylage are much easier to pack and feed. It is not wise to suddenly change at the competition as it has been known to cause disorders; again it must be introduced to the diet well in advance.

TIMING OF FEEDING

- Whenever possible, try to stick to your normal routine.
- Haynets during travel may help to settle a horse. It is not good feeding practice to deprive the gut of fibre for long periods of time. A small amount of roughage should be fed, even to a horse going cross-country.

ONE-DAY COMPETITIONS

Feed the normal concentrate breakfast. When travelling, this should be given an hour before departure. A haynet should be given during travel. The quantity fed will depend on the type of competition. The normal amount can be given for dressage and show jumping. If the horse is going cross-country the ration should be halved. The same principles apply when stabling at the competition.

During dressage and show jumping competitions, a small haynet can be given between classes. Haynets should be removed two to four hours in advance from horses that are going cross-country.

After cross-country the horse can be allowed to graze once fully recovered. A haynet should be given for the journey home.

THREE-DAY EVENTS

Feeding on cross-country day is a common cause for concern, so much so I have known people not feed at all, and reduce the ration the day before. This is likely to cause more of a problem. Always feed as normal the day before.

On cross-country day feed a small amount of hay/haylage (4.5 to 6.5kg/2 to 3lb) in the morning if your horse is not starting until the afternoon. If you have a morning start, the horse may have a pick of grass or a small handful early on.

At top-level competitions, energy requirements are high. Timing of concentrate feeds is more important. Aim to feed five hours before the start of phase A. This will provide maximum energy sources. If the feed is not eaten immediately it should be removed.

Feeding after the cross-country is as important. Giving a small concentrate feed first will help restore glucose levels and aid recovery. This should be given about an hour and half after exercise. This can be followed by a small amount of hay/haylage. The normal roughage and concentrate feed, containing supplements should be fed in the evening. It is normal for the horse to be a little fussy as he is likely to be tired and often sore. The feed should be left in over night and will usually be finished by morning.

PROBLEMS ASSOCIATED WITH FEEDING THE COMPETITION HORSE

Colic

Colic is the general term used to describe abdominal pain or 'tummy ache'. Any horse or pony may suffer from colic at any time. However, studies have shown that over 50% of cases are management related and may be prevented. There are many causes of colic, the most common in the competition horse being: diet, stress, change in routine and dehydration.

Colic can result in a problem affecting the stomach, small or large intestine, small colon, liver, spleen or kidney. The most common types of colic are:

- Impaction
- Spasmodic
- Surgical
- Tympanitic

It is important in caring for the horse that we recognize symptoms early, know how to act and try to prevent reccurrence.

SYMPTOMS

The horse will generally appear uncomfortable but symptoms may include:

- Rolling and thrashing.
- Lying down flat and very still.
- Frequently lying down and getting up.
- Frequently looking round at flanks.
- Kicking the belly.
- Digging the ground.
- Sweating.
- Increased temperature, pulse, respiration (TPR).
- Not eating.
- Lack of droppings.

IMMEDIATE ACTION/POINTS TO CONSIDER

- Remove all food.
- Take horse's temperature, pulse and respiration.
- A mild attack of colic may pass. Observe the horse for twenty minutes. If symptoms persist or become worse in this time, call the vet immediately.
- Frequent mild attacks should not be ignored.
- The horse should not be allowed to roll about and thrash in the stable as he may become cast or injure himself. To avoid this, move to a small paddock or arena.
- The horse can be left in the stable if he is standing or lying down quietly.
- Check he is not too hot or cold.
- Frequently check the TPR while waiting for the vet to arrive.

QUESTIONS THE VET WILL ASK

- When did the symptoms start?
- Does the horse have a history of colic?
- What he is being fed?
- Has the diet changed recently?
- When was he last fed?

- Is he drinking well?
- Are the droppings normal? When did he last pass droppings?
- When was he last exercised?
- Has there been a change in routine?
- When was he last wormed?
- When were the teeth last checked?

TREATMENT

This will depend on the type of colic. Mild spasmodic colic usually responds well to drugs. An impaction can usually be treated with drugs to relieve the pain and tubing the horse with liquid paraffin to lubricate and get the blockage moving. Surgical colic such as a twisted gut is much more serious and will require surgery. Unfortunately, this is not always a success and can prove fatal.

It is important to inform the vet of the horse's competition plans. It may be possible with a mild case to avoid administering drugs that have a lengthy withdrawal period.

Ensure you follow the vet's advice on after care.

PREVENTION ('Prevention is better than cure')

- Always treat colic seriously.
- Know your horse well and note any slight changes in routine and behaviour.
- Always follow the basic principles of watering and feeding.
- Follow a strict worming programme.
- Have teeth checked every six months.
- Feed a probiotic during periods when the horse is likely to become stressed or to have a change of routine.

Azoturia

This can also be known as Equine Rhabdomyolysis, Tying Up, Setfast or Monday morning disease. It is a painful condition affecting the muscle groups along the back and hind quarters, causing them to stiffen and seize up. It is similar to cramp. There are many causes but it is commonly related to the performance horse. It is important to recognize the symptoms early, know how to deal with the horse and try to prevent it recurring

CAUSES

- Diets containing small quantities of fibre and high levels of starch. This tends to cause digestive disorders and excitability. Both have shown to be factors contributing to azoturia.
- Not reducing rations on a day off or during periods of box rest.
- Dehydration and electrolyte imbalance.
- Insufficient warm up and cooling down before and after hard training.
- Fatigue.

SYMPTOMS

These will vary depending on the severity of the condition and include:
- The horse will generally look anxious and in pain.
- He may gradually stiffen or after standing still be unable to move.
- Sweating.
- Increased TPR.
- May pass reddish, brown urine.
- Muscles may appear swollen and be painful to the touch.

TREATMENT

- The vet must be called immediately.
- Keep the horse as comfortable as possible. Ensure he does not get cold.
- Do not attempt to move the horse. The vet will administer drugs to relieve the pain. It will then be necessary to transport the horse back to the stable.
- Blood tests will be taken to determine the severity. It is necessary to continue taking samples to monitor and ensure full recovery before work is resumed.
- The diet must consist of water and good quality roughage only until the horse is allowed out of the stable. When gentle exercise and turn out is allowed concentrates can be introduced slowly.

PREVENTION

- Avoid feeding high cereal diets.
- Feed fibre and oil as an alternative source of energy.
- Ensure the horse does not become dehydrated during travel and competition. When in doubt always seek veterinary advice.

- Always feed electrolytes during hard training, hot weather, travel and competition.
- Vitamin E and selenium are important antioxidants, helpful in healing and preventing muscle damage. They are ideal supplement for horses who are in hard work or prone to tying up.
- Always warm up and cool down well.
- Never work or compete your horse if you are in doubt about his health or level of fitness.

Respiratory disorders

Stabled horses are more at risk of respiratory disorders than horses living out at grass. This is primarily due to environment and what we feed them. COPD (Chronic obstructive pulmonary disease) otherwise known as RAO (Recurrent airway obstruction) is the most common occurring respiratory disease. It can affect any type of horse or pony. It is caused by an allergic reaction to mould spores present in feed, bedding, stables, indoor schools and horse boxes. When inhaled the spores irritate the airways and lungs, causing inflammation and a build up of mucus.

SYMPTOMS

- Coughing
- Nasal discharge
- Difficulty in breathing
- Poor performance

It is impossible to eliminate all mould from our horse's environment. We must however do our upmost to minimize them otherwise health and performance will be seriously inhibited.

PREVENTION

This not only relates to what we feed but also how we keep our horses.

- Stables must be well ventilated.
- Walls and ceilings should be dusted down at least once a month.
- Always use good quality, clean bedding. Avoid straw for hypersensitive horses. In my experience paper bedding has proved to be the most

suitable bed for the competition horse.

- Beware of shavings as poor quality can often contain more dust and mould spores than straw.
- Avoid deep litter systems as ammonia will irritate the respiratory tract.
- Avoid bedding down when the horse is in the stable.
- Do not stable allergic horses next to straw beds or storage barns.
- Provide as much turn out as possible.
- Avoid working on dusty surfaces.
- Provide as much ventilation during travel as possible.
- Always feed good quality feed stuffs.
- Allergic horses should be fed haylage or hay that is soaked for 20 minutes prior to feeding.
- There are many supplements available to help reduce the symptoms. Vitamins A, C and E work together as an important antioxidant to combat free radical damage, helping to reduce airway inflammation and reduce oxidative stress. Garlic, marshmallow root, coltsfoot leaves and liquorice root help reduce inflammation and encourage the expulsion of mucous.
- If symptoms persist it is advisable to seek veterinary advice.

CHAPTER 6
Fittening

Preparing a horse for competition entails a specialist training and fittening programme. The type and amount of work involved will vary, depending on the individual horse and the ultimate goal. In my experience, no two horses respond to work in the same way, therefore it is necessary to treat each horse as an individual. Fittening is similar to feeding, in that it becomes easier with experience and knowing your horse well.

This chapter aims to give you the basic guide lines on fittening. In my opinion it is a mistake to read a book that has set out a specific fittening

A healthy, fit horse

programme, and then try to follow it. It is unlikely it will suit your horse and you may end up doing more harm than good. What is more important is to know what you are aiming for and have knowledge of the type of work that is required to achieve it. Also being able to recognize that a particular programme is not having the desired effect, and knowing how to change it.

AIMS OF FITTENING

Increase fitness without over training

The majority of injuries occur as a result of training rather than competition. It may be during competition the horse is pushed that little bit harder and is the case of 'the last straw that broke the camel's back'. Hard training causes wear and tear to bones, muscles, tendons and ligaments. Many horses fail to reach top level due to soundness problems, not lack of ability. Fittening and training should entail as little work as possible to reach the desired result. Horses that require a lot of fittening work tend to break down much quicker and have a shorter competition career. Achieving the right balance can be difficult and under no circumstances should short cuts be taken. An unfit horse is just as likely to injure himself. It is through experience with different horses and training methods that you will become more confident and competent at the job.

Reduce risk of injury

Fittening produces changes in both the musculoskeletal and cardiovascular systems. It is essential to stress the system to improve fitness, without over stressing which will lead to injury.

Consideration must also be taken into training methods to suit the strengths of individual horses. The type of surface you work on also has a big impact on keeping a horse sound. Injury can be minimized by early recognition that your horse is not coping with the programme. This may be felt when training or by noticing physical changes when checking your horse over.

Improve performance and competition results

A fittening programme should not only aim to improve physical fitness. Training is required to improve the performance of the horse. This will obviously vary depending on the competition goal. Improving the skill of the horse decreases energy demands both physically and mentally. This will help delay the onset of fatigue, which contributes greatly to the cause of injury.

Improve psychological condition

Working a horse hard often results in him becoming 'sour'. Work programmes should vary. The horse should not find every day a challenge. A horse that is unhappy in his work will soon become stressed. This will lead to ill health and poor performance.

CONSIDERATIONS WHEN PLANNING A PROGRAMME

Ultimate goal

When planning a competition season you tend to have an ultimate goal in mind. This may be a certain level you want to achieve or a specific competition such as a championship or a three-day event. Plan your fittening programme working back from this. You must know what is required of your horse and how fit he needs to be. Knowing how long it will take to achieve this can be straight forward if you know the horse well. A new horse is more difficult to assess. It is advisable in this case to allow extra time. It is much safer to give an easy week to an over fit horse than having to work your horse too hard. It is also likely at some point your horse will miss a week's work due to injury or illness. Bad weather may also cause set backs. Again this should be taken into consideration and ample time allowed.

Type of horse

The type or breed has a great impact on the choice and amount of work the horse requires. In general terms the thoroughbred will take less fittening than a half bred horse. As well as fittening, it is important to consider training. The thoroughbred may be very 'clean in the wind' and require minimal fast work but have a weak top line needing more dressage and hill work to build it up.

Age

A young horse or a horse that has never been fit before will take a lot longer than a fit horse coming back from a holiday. It is thought that it takes two years for a horse to reach peak fitness from scratch. Therefore competition demands should not be too high in this period otherwise it may result in breakdown. It is often better for an older horse, who suffers from arthritic conditions, not to be given a complete rest. Keeping him in light work during a holiday will prevent stiffness. The old horse should not be allowed to get fat, as this will require a harder fittening programme to bring him back.

Period of rest

The longer a horse has had off, the longer it will take to get him fit again. A fit horse that has had a six week holiday will lose very little fitness. In my opinion, unless a horse has been injured, he should not be off for any longer than this. A horse who is allowed to become fat and unfit will require much more work. This is added wear and tear on the legs.

Injury

A horse coming back from injury may require a slower fittening programme. Always follow your vet's advice and monitor the injury closely.

BRINGING THE HORSE UP FROM GRASS

Before starting to work your horse again it is important to ensure he is sound and healthy. The week before you start your fittening programme should be spent preparing him both physically and mentally.

If the horse has been turned out full time, he may not adjust well to suddenly being stabled 24 hours a day. Bring the horse in for a short period during the day and turn him out again over night. The period he is in for can increase each day. It may be possible during the early stages of fittening to continue turning the horse out over night, if this makes him more relaxed.

The digestive system will need to adjust if the horse has been living off grass only. Start by introducing small amounts of hay or haylage. A small, non-heating concentrate feed can also be given. The feed should be increased gradually along with the fittening programme. If your horse is prone to digestive upsets, feeding a prebiotic may help the system adjust.

The feet must be in good order before the work programme commences. The farrier should examine the balance of the feet closely. Suitable shoes for road work should be fitted. It is advisable to have grip or road studs.

The teeth should be examined if they have not been checked in the last six months. Worming and vaccinations should be up to date.

The horse should be groomed to remove mud and grease. This will cause a problem when tack is applied, especially if the coat is heavy. The fit of the saddle should be checked as the horse may have changed shape.

If you have the use of a horsewalker it is advantageous to walk the horse for half an hour a day with a saddle and breastplate on. This will get a young horse accustomed to the girth again. It will also help to harden the skin on the back and girth area.

TYPES OF WORK

The type of work necessary will vary depending on the competition you are preparing for. All fittening programmes should follow a similar procedure for the first four to six weeks, unless the horse has had a long time off or is coming back from injury. It is after this that specialized training and conditioning for each discipline will need to be considered.

Slow work

The first stage of any fittening programme will involve a period of walking and trotting. A horse that is returning to work following a short break will require approximately four weeks of hacking in walk and trot. A horse that has suffered injury or has had a long period of rest may require longer. If the horse is carrying excess fat, it should remain in slow work until weight has been reduced.

Slow work gradually develops the structural strength of bone, muscle, tendon and ligament, to prepare for the added stress of dressage training, galloping and jumping.

During the first two weeks the horse should remain in walk only, building up from 45 minutes to an hour and increasing to approximately 75 minutes by the end of the second week. Care must be taken to ensure the back doesn't become sore as the muscles must become accustomed to carrying the weight of the rider. Trot can be introduced in the third week. Trotting up a slight incline will help reduce concussion. It is not advisable to trot on the flat or down hill as it is jarring on the joints and the horse will be at risk of slipping. Trot work can be increased during week four.

Trotting on the road may not always be of benefit. In my experience, horses with very flat feet do not cope well with the concussion. In some cases it will lead to lameness. It may have the same effect on an older horse with arthritic joints. Walking for longer periods or including hill work will prepare the horse for fast work. Hacking will not benefit the horse greatly if he is backward and lazy. The walk should be active and over tracking. I tend to allow a long rein to encourage the horse to go forward. When trotting, the contact should be taken up and the horse ridden in an outline. Trotting up hill is ideal for lengthening the stride and working on the medium trot. Lazy horses may benefit from hacking in company.

As the work is increased, it is important to ensure the horse is coping with the programme. Towards the end of a hack he should be relaxed but still walking out. A tired horse will be reluctant to go forward, the stride may be shorter and stumbling may occur. Unsteady head carriage or grabbing at the rein may indicate sore back muscles. In this case it is advisable to dismount and lead the horse home. Work must be reduced until the horse is coping well. The diet may also need adjusting to provide more energy.

If on the other hand, the horse is returning from work very fresh and looking well, it may indicate the work is insufficient and the fittening programme can be moved on a little quicker.

By the end of week four you should start to notice changes in the horse's appearance. Muscle condition will quickly return if the horse has been rested for a short period. A young horse will be slower to develop but slight changes should be noticeable.

Hill work

Hill work not only has a great impact on conditioning but also holds several advantages.

- Working the horse up hill increases the intensity of exercise, therefore distance can be reduced. This saves time and is less wear and tear on the legs.
- Walking and trotting up hill, helps to reduce fat and develop body muscle. To enable the muscle to build up correctly, the horse must be ridden 'up to the bridle' in an outline suitable for the level of training.
- Hill work also conditions the cardiovascular system. Even walking up a steep hill will increase the pulse and respiration. Trot work up hill should be introduced gradually, always monitoring the recovery rate.
- Reduces the level of stress put on the legs, especially when trotting on the road.
- In my opinion, hill work is an invaluable part of any conditioning programme. The effect it has on both the musculoskeletal and cardio-vascular systems should not be under estimated. I remember preparing a horse for a three star three-day event, during a very hot, dry period. The ground was very hard and not ideal for canter work. Not having the use of an all weather surface, I replaced much of the interval training with hill work. I arrived at the event, unsure that the horse was fit enough for the competition. In fact she proved to be fitter than ever, at the end of the cross-country the vets commented on how impressed they were with her recovery rate.

Fast work

'Fast work' or canter work is the most common method of conditioning the cardiovascular system. The aim being to develop the strength of the heart, to increase oxygen delivery to the muscles, which in return increases stamina, delaying the onset of fatigue. This is achieved by improving the horse's aerobic capacity, enabling him to work for longer without using anaerobic metabolism. To understand this, it is important to know the difference between aerobic and anaerobic metabolism. **Aerobic exercise** produces energy by using oxygen. **Anaerobic exercise** produces energy without the use of oxygen.

Aerobic exercise is much more efficient and unlike anaerobic exercise does not accumulate lactic acid in the muscles, which causes fatigue and discomfort, or more seriously Azoturia

Aerobic metabolism usually occurs at a heart rate of up to 170 to 180 beats per minute. When the horse is pushed beyond this, or energy sources are depleted, he will reach the anaerobic threshold. This will result in a build up of lactic acid in the muscles causing him to tire quickly, often resulting in poor performance or injury. Training the horse aerobically will increase the anaerobic threshold, allowing him to work for longer using oxygen and delaying the onset of fatigue.

Work performed aerobically.

- Hacking
- Dressage
- Long distance riding
- Lungeing/Long reining
- Roads and Tracks phase of a three-day event

Most competitive work involves both aerobic and anaerobic exercise

- Eventing
- Show jumping
- Racing
- Polo
- Endurance races

Canter work can be introduced between weeks 4 and 8, when the horse is coping well with hacking for 1 to $1\frac{1}{2}$ hours, walking and trotting up hills. Again, cantering up a slight incline is more beneficial. As the horse gets fitter, it is more of an advantage to canter up hill. The horse would be required to do three times the distance on the flat than he would up a hill. This is a serious increase in wear and tear on the legs.

METHODS OF CANTERING

This will depend on the type of horse and facilities available to you. The ideal is to use a good all weather or turf gallop of 1 to 1$^{1}/_{2}$ miles, with a gradual incline, becoming steeper for the last half mile. In my experience this is suitable for fittening work up to three and four star three-day event level, without over working and placing too much strain on the legs. The equivalent of working twice up the gallop would require you to do three by eight minute canters around a flat field. Repeatedly, this would cause strain, especially if the ground is hard. When preparing for top level competition, I would advise spending extra time and money on finding suitable training facilities. Before using a gallop the horse should have reached light to medium fitness. For example, Novice one-day event fit.

When using a field, it should be a suitable size to enable you to keep a rhythm and not have to keep pulling up on every turn. The ground should not be too hard or soft when cantering for long periods. In firm conditions, a good covering of grass will help reduce concussion.

SPEED AND DISTANCE

When introducing canter work it is important to have a good idea of the speed you need to be working at. This will depend on the type and level of competition you are aiming for. Speed is an important factor contributing to the occurrence of injuries. Therefore, it is not advisable to work faster than necessary. An experienced competition rider will have a feel for speed; a less experienced person should set up 100 metre (110 yard) markers around the field and use a stop watch to guide them.

It can be difficult to estimate distance when cantering around a field without the use of markers. A more common and practical method is to time the canters. 'Interval training' is very popular. It involves a period of work followed by a short recovery period, then a second period of work, this can be followed by a third and forth. It is an easy method to follow, as the fitness develops the distance and speed increases and the rest period decreases. The recovery rate must be noted during the rest period, in which the horse must be kept walking. This can be done by the use of a heart rate monitor, or a more practical method is to monitor the respiration. As you become more experienced and get to know your horse better you will quickly be able to assess his condition through feel. If at any point during the exercise the horse becomes stressed or appears to struggle, the work should be stopped. This could be due to fatigue or injury and the horse must be monitored closely. As mentioned previously, the disadvantage of this type of canter work as opposed to using a gallop is the horse is required to do a lot more work to achieve the same result.

At the stage when canter work is introduced, the horse must be coping well with the present stage of fittening. He must not be carrying excessive amounts of weight or showing any signs of injury. Slow cantering will have already been introduced during dressage and show jump schooling sessions. Hill work will have also helped prepare him. The first canter session could consist of three by three minute sessions around a field, with a two to three minute break in between. Alternately, once up a 1.6 to 2.4 km (1 to 1^1/$_2$ mile) long gallop track. The speed when cantering around a field should be carried out at approximately 400 to 450 metres (440 to 500 yards) per minute. The speed on the gallop should start at this and gradually allow the horse to quicken towards the last 800 metres (^{1}/$_2$ mile). At no point during any canter work should the horse be allowed to canter off the bridle with a free rein. A tired horse will quickly become unbalanced; keeping a contact on the mouth will help to maintain balance and co-ordination, reducing the risk of injury.

It is important during all stages of fittening to monitor the recovery rate. A horse getting fit for the first time or following a long period of rest will be much slower to respond. The canter work should progress each week, keeping the peak fitness target in mind. The condition of the horse must be monitored closely along with signs of physical and mental stress. As I mentioned earlier, I do not feel it appropriate to set out cantering programmes for you to follow. I think it is important to work individually with each horse. If in doubt it is advisable to seek advice from your trainer or a knowledgeable person who knows your horse.

It is usual to canter the horse twice weekly, competitions counting as a session. The system requires three days to recover fully from a hard work out, therefore it is ideal to canter every fourth day. Remember, as with any work, do not do more than is required. A thoroughbred horse may require much less than this.

When aiming for a top level competition, such as a three or four star three-day event, it is important not to over do the stamina work too close to the competition as this depletes energy reserves. Aim to peak the stamina work around four weeks before the event. From then on work more on quality rather than quantity. The canters should become shorter but include sprints. This will continue to improve cardiovascular and muscular fitness without taking too much out of the horse. When the horse starts canter work, energy requirements will increase. Diets should be altered in quantity and type of feed to suit the individual requirements.

Dressage training

Dressage training or working the horse on the flat has two main values:

- Development of muscles
- Development of skill

Development of muscles is an important part of any conditioning programme. Different types of work will strengthen different muscle groups. The stronger the horse becomes, the easier he is able to perform. When working on the flat, the horse should be encouraged to work in **self carriage**. The outline he takes and the demands put on him must follow his level of training and fitness. This work strengthens and develops the top line, abdominal and hind quarter muscles. It also helps to balance and co-ordinate the horse. It is not only the dressage or event horse that benefit from this, but any type of performance horse.

Not all competition activities require the same element of flat work skill. For example, the race horse requires very little, the grand prix dressage horse requires a lot. Show jumpers and event horses tend to be much more successful if they are trained well on the flat. Riding to a single fence is easy; most people have difficulty riding a course. This is usually due to poor control on the flat. Riding a well schooled horse makes it much easier to adjust the pace, ride turns and lines more accurately, enabling a course to be ridden well.

Each horse should be assessed individually to decide on the amount of training required. In general I feel dressage and event horses are often over trained. As with fast work, this can also develop soundness problems. It is very unnatural for a horse to go round and round in circles for an hour every day and can be very unforgiving on the joints. **Quality is better than Quantity.** Working a horse productively for 30 to 40 minutes is more beneficial than trotting and cantering round aimlessly for an hour.

Flat work can be introduced into the fittening programme as early as week three if the horse has come back from a short break. An unfit horse will need a few more weeks of road work. Introduce 20 minutes work to begin with. Keep the work basic to start and avoid small circles during the first week as this is added strain. Trot work should be 'rising', until the back muscles have properly adjusted to carrying a rider again. Canter may also need to be done in light seat. Listen to what your horse is telling you. The horse does not forget what he has previously learnt during a holiday. If he is resistant and argumentative over something that he would usually accept, it is likely he is feeling discomfort and not yet able to cope with your demands.

Build up the work weekly, the amount you need to do will depend on your goal and how the horse is responding both physically and mentally. Too much flat work can be very demanding; over working will lead to injury and cause the horse to become 'sour'. Vary the type of schooling by including lungeing and long reining. It is also possible to work the horse as productively when hacking down the road. It may help the horse psychologically to have a change of scene. I often school horses around the cross-country field or up and down hills, rather than in the arena. This is excellent for young horses as it works on balance and co-ordination. It also exposes them to open spaces and 'spooky' situations, improving confidence and preparing for competition environment.

Always try to work on a good surface. Grass is ideal when the ground is not too hard or boggy. Avoid working on a prepared surface that is very deep as it becomes very tiring for the horse and may cause strain. Remember, the more care taken, the longer the horse will last.

Jumping

The aims of jump training are:

- Develop strength and muscles
- Develop skill
- Develop confidence
- Improve mental attitude

Jump training is not a necessary part of all conditioning programmes. It may not always be of benefit if the horse does not enjoy doing it due to lack of ability or confidence. A horse that is expected to jump in competition will need to train in order to develop both physically and mentally.

Dressage, hacking and hill work prepare the muscles for jumping. The hind quarter muscles must be strong to propel the horse off the ground in take off. The neck and shoulder muscles must be developed to balance and carry a horse on landing, to reduce the risk of injury to the fore leg. Jumping will help to develop these muscles but will also add considerable strain to the legs if done too frequently. Therefore it should not be the sole method of conditioning the show jumper. Continued hacking, hill work and dressage will be of more benefit.

Jump training should be aimed more at developing skill and confidence. A good natural jumper will require very little, often too much can have a negative affect. A confident horse may become less careful the more he does. Gymnastic jumping usually benefits most horses in their technique. It can also improve confidence and teach the horse to think quickly and get himself out of trouble.

The young horse will need to be introduced to colours and fillers. This is best done around a small course rather than a grid, as it may cause the horse to back off too much and lose confidence.

Course riding tends to be more beneficial for rider practice rather than training the horse. It is usually a problem with the flat work that causes difficulties when putting fences together. Some horses do however learn from jumping around a course as it teaches them to stay 'switched on'. The horse must land and look for the next fence, not land and want to pull up. This often applies to young or backward thinking horses. Cross-country schooling develops confidence and skill. It is also beneficial to the cardio-vascular system and should count as a fast work session in your conditioning programme. It is usual to take the event horse schooling a few times before they are introduced to competition. This gives them the opportunity to see a variety of fences such as water, ditches and banks. It also teaches them to jump from a more forward pace than show jump speed. Most experienced horses also benefit from a school prior to the first event of the season. This may also apply to hunters and team chasers.

During a normal conditioning programme, show jump training is introduced between weeks six and eight, or sooner with the mature horse. If the horse is returning from injury it is advisable to follow your vet's advice. By week eight it should be possible to go to show jump competitions and cross-country schooling.

Other horses such as dressage or endurance may benefit from jumping as a variation in their work programme.

As with any work, jump training must not be over done. In many cases it is the rider who needs the practice more than the horse; this is where the one horse rider is at a disadvantage compared to someone who has a string of horses. Jumping should not be done for the sake of it but as a productive exercise to improve confidence and technique. Relevant exercises should be chosen to suit horse and rider. If all is going well in competition it is often not necessary to jump in between shows or events.

It can often be a mistake to jump the day before a competition. If the session goes badly, both horse and rider will lack confidence and feel negative towards competing. Often confidence is a more important factor than skill. Jumping earlier in the week allows for another session later if things go badly.

LOOSE JUMPING

In my opinion, loose jumping has its benefits for all types of horses. It improves technique and confidence by allowing the horse to work things out for himself, without the help or interference of a rider. It also enables you to assess a horse's jumping ability, as it will show his natural style over a fence, which can often be influenced greatly by a rider. It also shows how the horse reacts when he meets a jump incorrectly, and how he gets himself out of trouble. This is very important for the event horse, point to pointer and steeplechaser.

Loose jumping should not be introduced too early as it is quite demanding on the cardiovascular system. The horse must be coping well with trotting up hills and also with schooling on the flat. It can also be used to exercise a horse with a girth gall or saddle rub, or reduce freshness before riding.

Lungeing/long reining

This improves muscle development and develops skill. Lungeing can be used as an alternative form of exercise. This could be to add variety to the work, reduce freshness prior to riding, or to work the horse without tack if he is suffering from a sore mouth, back or girth gall.

Lungeing and long reining can also improve muscle development and to some degree skill. In this case the horse must work in an outline with the assistance of side reins or other suitable gadgets.

It can be introduced into the conditioning programme at the same stage as dressage training. Gadgets should not be used to 'force' the horse into an outline he is not ready to take. This will lead to discomfort and soreness in the muscles, causing resistance and possibly a setback in the training programme. Sessions should not be longer than twenty minutes to begin with. The circle should remain no smaller than 15 metres (16$^1/_2$ yards). As the horse develops the session can build up to forty minutes and the work become more demanding, varying the paces and size of circle. The horse can be encouraged to work in a more advanced outline as he becomes stronger.

From a safety point of view, it may be necessary to lunge the horse prior to riding. This is often the case with a young horse. At this stage in training the horse is not very fit, therefore should not be lunged for more than fifteen minutes on a large circle.

Swimming

I want to briefly mention swimming as I have used it for several horses with great success. It has a tremendous impact on both muscular and cardiovascular conditioning, without concussive stress on the limbs. This is useful when fittening horses with chronic limb problems or rehabilitating an injured horse.

The competition horse suffers largely from tendon and ligament injury. When brought back to top level competition they are at high risk of recurrence. As mentioned earlier, it is more likely to be the fittening work that causes breakdown than the competition itself. Combining swimming into the programme allows the amount of fast work to be reduced.

Individual requirements

As a guide, these are the types of work the following conditioning programmes could include.

DISCIPLINE	NECESSARY WORK	OPTIONAL LIKELY TO BENEFIT	OPTIONAL
Dressage	Slow work Dressage training Lungeing Long reining	Hacking Hill work Fast work	Jumping Loose jumping Swimming
Show jumping	Slow work Hill work Dressage training Jump training	Slow canters Lungeing Loose jumping	Swimming
Eventing	Slow work Hill work Dressage training Jump training XC schooling Fast work	Lungeing Loose jumping	Swimming
Hunter Team Chaser	Slow work Hill work Fast work Lungeing	Dressage training Jump training XC schooling Lungeing	Swimming
Endurance	Slow work Hill work Fast work	Dressage training	Jumping Lungeing Loose jumping Swimming

CHECKS TO BE MADE DURING CONDITIONING

One of the most important responsibilities in taking care of the horse is recognizing problems, both physically and mentally. The horse will change in many ways during the conditioning programme, from been brought up from grass to reaching peak fitness. It is important to recognize the difference between a horse responding well to his work and one not coping with the demands.

Legs/feet

The most common injuries occur in the legs and feet. It is important to recognize symptoms early if the problem is to remain minimal. You must be familiar with all normal lumps and bumps on each individual horse's legs. Each morning, before exercise the feet and legs must be checked for heat, swelling and pain.

Heat in the feet or swelling in the joints is a common symptom of stress, often as a result of concussion. Anti-inflammatory treatment and reduction in work will help relieve this if treated early. If symptoms persist it is advisable to consult your vet. Heat and swelling in the tendon area is more likely to be caused by a strain, usually following jumping or fast work. Work must be stopped immediately; ice packs or cold hosing will reduce inflammation. The vet must be called to assess the extent of the damage.

Back

During the early stages of conditioning it is not unusual for the horse to suffer from a sore back. Skin soreness can be detected when running your hands over the skin, or by the horse objecting to being groomed in the area.

Muscular soreness may occur during any stage of conditioning, usually as a result of over training. Reduction in work and anti-inflammatory treatment should help. As with humans, some horses suffer from chronic muscular pain. I have found that regular physiotherapy and the use of magnetic rugs helps to relieve the pain.

Condition

It is important that the horse maintains the right amount of condition throughout the fittening programme. If possible weigh and condition score weekly. Observe the horse both in the stable and under saddle, it can present a very different picture. When standing relaxed, the horse will often appear much fatter than he actually is. If the horse is losing weight rapidly he may need the diet adjusting, this is often a sign of over training.

Temperament

The horse's attitude will give a lot away as to how he is coping. He should maintain a healthy appetite; reluctance to eat is a common symptom of stress. In general the horse should appear bright and alert. If he is looking dull and lethargic it may indicate that he is tired. He may need his feed increasing and the work reducing until he is feeling brighter.

CAUSES OF POOR PERFORMANCE

Over training

Over training is a common cause for poor performance. The horse that is constantly subjected to high demands of training becomes fatigued as energy supplies are depleted. If the pressure is not reduced it will lead to resistance and mentally the horse will not want to perform.

Work must be reduced immediately to allow energy supplies to be restored. It may be worth discussing your horse's diet with a nutritionist, to ensure you are feeding a balanced diet. Check the horse is drinking sufficient amounts by using water buckets rather than automatic drinkers.

The horse may benefit mentally by being turned out in the field. There should be an improvement within a week. If not it is advisable to discuss with your vet as the problem may be more serious.

Ill health/injury

Unfortunately our horses cannot tell us when they are not feeling too well or they are in pain. They do not have to be hopping lame or coughing to not feel 100%. This can often be the reason for poor performance. During slow, easy exercise we may not detect a difference. When the horse is asked to work hard or compete, performance is not up to scratch. Quite often we do not recognize this as being a sign of pain or ill health but we put it down to bad behaviour or riding. In racing, blood testing is used more frequently to monitor health and fitness. If a horse runs a bad race, the first thing the trainer will do is consult the vet. Blood testing is expensive and many people cannot afford to use it. It is not always necessary if we take notice of what our horses are telling us. A consistent horse will not suddenly lose form unless something is inhibiting performance.

Lack of ability

Not all humans are destined to become top athletes. This also applies to the horse. Some are simply more talented than others. This is often due to breeding, type and having good conformation to suit the job. However we often see horses with all the right attributes failing to make anything, and horses with very little going for them reaching the top. This is purely through having the right temperament, good management and training.

It is important to recognize during training when a horse has reached his limit. Some will make it quite clear by refusing to carry on. Others are much more generous in temperament and will struggle on, but performance is not always consistent. Forcing a horse to perform at a level he is not capable of is unfair and is most likely to end in bad temperament and injury.

CHAPTER 7
Tack and Equipment

Choosing the correct tack and equipment for your horse can be very difficult. With such a wide range available it is hard to know where to start. As with the fashion industry, saddlery and horse clothing go through trends. Often people buy a piece of equipment because it is the 'in thing', regardless of their horse's needs.

This chapter discusses the use and fit of the more commonly used competition saddlery and equipment. Badly fitting tack can often contribute to poor performance. However buying a new bit or saddle does not train your horse or improve your riding, this may also need attention.

BRIDLE

LEATHER
Must be good quality. Feel strong but supple.

STITCHING
All buckles must be well stitched and not coming away in any area.

SIZE
Pony, cob and full are the three standard sizes.

FIT
When fitted with a snaffle bridle the cheek pieces should fasten half way down. This allows the option of going higher or lower if a different type of bit is used.

BROWBAND
Should lie flat without pulling tight across the head or pinching the ears.

THROATLASH
When fastened allow four fingers at the jaw. Double check it is not too tight when the head is flexed.

SNAFFLE BIT
Should be fixed evenly to both cheek pieces, sitting straight in the mouth. It should be high enough not to interfere with the tushes, but not so high that it is opening the mouth and causing discomfort. A few wrinkles in the corner of the mouth are usually a good guide. The bit must be a suitable width; 63mm ($^1/_4$ inch) clearance at each side is more than ample. The thickness of the bit inside the mouth should also be considered.

Competion bridle
Should suit the horse. The thickness of the leather should relate to the size of the head. Rolled browbands and nosebands are more flattering. Choose a colour to suit your horse. Dark brown or black suits dark brown, black or grey horses. Lighter leather looks better on bays and chestnuts.

When buying a bridle for competition use only it is advisable to try it out at home beforehand. The competition is not the time to discover the bridle does not fit. More holes can be made but is not often done well when in a hurry. Use the bridle for a few weeks until it is well broken in. It then can be saved for competition.

If you are intending to compete in several disciplines, you may use different bits for each phase. It is useful to have separate bridles for this. There can be a big difference in the size of bridle required for a gag than that of your snaffle. It makes changing tack much easier especially when eventing and there is often little time between each phase.

Work bridles

These are useful to have to save your competition tack. The quality does not have to be as good but the condition and stitching must be sound. Nylon bridles may not look the part but are ideal for everyday use. As well as being labour saving they withstand wet weather much more than leather.

Araes to check for badly fitting briddles

- Around the ears.
- Noseband area (will be discussed in more detail).
- Corners of the mouth. This can be due to the bit being too small and pinching or having a sharp edge.
- Bars of the mouth due to the bit being too big or hanging too low.
- Bit injuries can also be caused by bad riding.

TREATMENT

- Remove the cause of the problem.
- In the case of a skin rub the area should be left clear until the soreness has gone and the skin is no longer pink.
- Protection can then be used until the hair grows back – this can be done by wrapping a piece of soft material around the leather.
- In the case of a sore mouth the horse should not wear a bit until it is completely healed. Ride in a bitless bridle or lunge in a cavesson
- In my experience the use of Vaseline does not help to heal the mouth, but makes it more prone to cracking. It may help to prevent certain types of bits rubbing by providing lubrication to the corner of the mouth.
- In some cases rubber bit guards may help.

NOSEBANDS

Cavesson

This is the mildest type of noseband usually worn for show. It should sit one to two fingers below the cheek bones, depending on the length of the head. It is fastened snugly at the back of the jaw, giving little restriction. It can be tightened to prevent the horse opening the jaw. The 'crank' type fastening doubles back on itself to enable it to be tightened more. This is often used in conjunction with the double bridle where no other noseband is permitted.

Flash

This is a cavesson noseband with a loop stitched on to the front. A strap is passed through the loop and fastened below the bit.

ACTION

Prevents the horse opening the mouth and evading the bit.

FIT

So often seen incorrectly fitted. The cavesson part of the noseband must be fastened first. It should sit higher than the plain cavesson, just below the cheek bones. It must be secured firmly to prevent it being pulled down by the lower strap. The lower strap is fastened below the bit, behind the jaw. This can be done as firmly as necessary.

Flash noseband incorrectly fitted

Correctly fitted flash noseband

Drop

ACTION

Prevents opening the mouth and crossing the jaw.

FIT

It has a single nosepiece which sits lower on the face and fastens below the bit. There is a danger of fitting it too low and restricting the breathing. Ensure the nose piece is always sitting on bone. It is then tightened accordingly.

The drop noseband

Grakle

ACTION

More effective than the flash or drop as it works on a wider area of the jaw.

The Grakle noseband

FIT

The noseband has a circular piece that sits on the centre of the face. It has two straps which pass through this forming a figure of eight around the nose. One strap fastens above the bit and the other below the bit. The Mexican Grakle is designed to allow the top strap to fasten much higher, similar to the top strap of a lunge cavesson. This gives greater restriction to the jaw. The top strap should be done up first. The central nosepiece should then be raised as high as possible, this must then be held in place while the lower strap is secured under the bit. Both straps can then be tightened as necessary. The noseband must not be worn loosely fitted as the central nosepiece will slip down and be ineffective.

Ill fitting

Any of the nosebands which I have mentioned may rub if not fitted correctly. The Grakle or flash will rub if fitted too close to the cheek bones. You should avoid lower strap buckles fastening over the mouth and bear in mind that nosebands fastened very tight may rub the jaw bone. As with other bridle sores, remove the cause and protect until healed.

REINS

Different types of reins are suitable for different disciplines and these are described below. Safety is important whatever the occasion. Stitching and fastenings must be checked regularly and if in doubt not used. The reins must be a suitable length and width for the intended purpose.

Dressage

- Narrow plain leather.
- Narrow plaited leather to provide more grip.
- Rubber inside, leather outside.
- Billet or buckle fastening.
- With a double bridle the bridoon rein will often be slightly wider than the curb.

Show jumping

- Rubber covered.
- Leather plaited.
- Webbing.
- Billet or buckle fastening.
- Rein stops if a running martingale is worn.

Cross-country/Hunting

- Rubber covered leather provides the best grip still allowing the rein to be slipped.
- Buckle or loop fastening (billets are not strong enough).
- Rein stops if martingale is worn.

MARTINGALES

The purpose of the martingale is not to keep the head down, but to prevent the horse from raising his head above the point of control.

Running Martingale

ACTION

Discourages the horse from raising his head by applying pressure to the bars of the mouth. Can however have an adverse effect if the horse doesn't accept the action.

USES

Young horses; when hacking fit or fresh horses; show jumping and cross-country horses that tend to raise their head coming into the jump and for novice riders who can use it to provide a neck strap.

FIT

The neck strap should not be restricting in any way. Allow for a good hand's width. The strap to the girth should give plenty of clearance without the risk of a leg getting caught in it when jumping. The rings of the martingale should lie flat and the reins must pass up through them, to avoid a twist.

The length of the martingale will vary slightly depending on its use. It must never be fitted so short that it is applying pressure to the mouth when the head is in a normal position. A good guide is that the rings should follow the length of the neck and reach the top of the jaw, or when drawn back will reach the wither. The martingale must not be fitted too short for cross-country. When in trouble the horse uses his neck as a fifth leg, he cannot do so if restricted by the martingale.

DISADVANTAGES

The martingale can interfere with the contact. Avoid using when schooling on the flat. If used when doing grid work it can restrict the use of the head and neck, preventing the horse from using himself over the jump. The use of the 'opening rein' is restricted. This is invaluable when training the young horse or riding difficult 'nappy' horses.

Standing Martingale

ACTION

It has the same uses as the running martingale but acts in a different way. Rather than acting on the reins it has a single loop that attaches to the cavesson noseband. When the horse raises his head pressure is applied to the nose, and not the mouth which some horses prefer. It is more suitable for 'nappy' horses that require more control as it allows the use of the 'opening rein'.

FIT

It should not be fitted to force the head down but to come in to action when the head comes up. The strap should follow the length of the neck and jaw to reach the noseband, not directly from the chest to the noseband.

DISADVANTAGES

It is more restricting, therefore some horses may panic at the feel of it. This should never be used for cross-country as it can restrict the use of the neck

Standing maringale

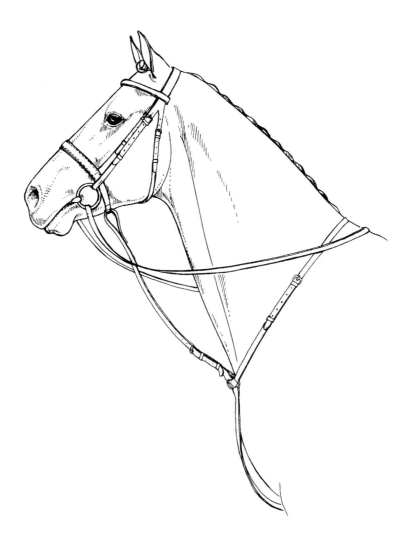

and the horse may feel restricted when jumping. This can cause him to become hollow and tight in the back over the fence.

BREASTPLATES

Worn to prevent the saddle from slipping back. Essential for racing, jumping, hunting or cross-country. As a horse becomes fit his body will change shape. His tummy will disappear and he will become very lean and even the best fitting saddle will slip back.

It is also useful for a novice rider to hold on to when jumping to prevent pulling the horse in the mouth.

Hunting

The hunting breastplate looks very tidy on the horse but is the least effective. I prefer to use it for dressage and show jumping, or for less fit horses competing at a lower level cross-country. It can double up as a martingale by using an attachment. It must then be fitted as a martingale and will have little effect on keeping the saddle in place.

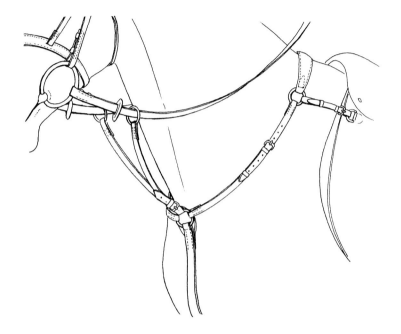

Hunting breastplate with martingale attachment

Aintree

More effective than the hunting breastplate. A thick strap passes around the front of the chest and fastens directly to the girth straps. It is advisable to use an elastic one when galloping and jumping. They are commonly fitted too low and are at risk of interfering with the shoulder action. The loop must be placed over one girth strap only to prevent it slipping down. The neck strap should be secured high enough, giving the shoulder free range of movement.

For maximum security at a three-day event I tend to use both breastplates together. The Aintree is fitted first; the hunting is then put on top. The martingale attachment can be used if needed.

ILL FITTING

The Aintree breastplate is the most likely to rub. It can become very tight during a gallop or on a cross-country round. Horses that are clipped and

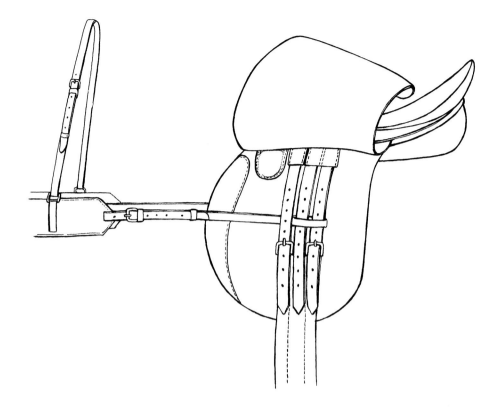

sweat a lot tend to be more badly effected. Horses with long coats may have the hair rubbed off and be left with bald patches: this tends to be less sore but is unsightly. It does not work to loosen the breastplate as this will allow the saddle to move more and the breastplate will still tighten. It may be necessary to cover with sheepskin. Girth covers work well by cutting two small slits to thread the neck strap through.

FOREGIRTH

This is used to prevent the saddle slipping forward. More commonly used in dressage. It consists of a surcingle with a metal arch. This is placed in front of the saddle. It must be secured before the saddle is put in place.

BITS

Often when a horse is performing badly the first thing the rider does is change the bit. This may make a difference for a day or two but the problem soon returns. It is rare the horse does not go well because he doesn't like the feel of what is in his mouth. It is more likely he is feeling discomfort. If this is not identified the problem will only get worse.

Reasons for discomfort

- Teeth problems.
- Badly fitting tack.
- Lameness/ill health.
- Demands of training.
- Rider skill.

The above should be considered before changing the bit.

The choice of bits available is never ending. They do however fit into certain categories.

- Snaffle
- Curb
- Double
- Gag
- Combination
- Bitless

Each category has many variations including the material it is made from, the type of mouth piece, the type of cheek piece and the length of shank.

Fitting

Most bits fit as previously discussed when fitting the snaffle bridle. Some do need slight adjustment.

SNAFFLE GAG

Used for jumping and cross-country. Fits a hole higher than the normal snaffle. The leather cheek pieces must be well oiled to allow them to run smoothly through the bit.

THREE RING GAG/AMERICAN GAG

May need to be raised more than the snaffle gag. When the reins are taken up the cheek pieces must not become loose and move forward towards the eye. This will happen if the bit is too low.

BITLESS/COMBINATION

Must not be fitted too low as it will interfere with the breathing. The nose must be checked for rubs and sores. In cases where the noseband has been very tight, a swelling may appear on the bony part of the nose. The bridle should not be used again until the swelling has subsided. The nose piece should then be covered in sheepskin.

DOUBLE BRIDLE

The bits must be a suitable size for the mouth. The bridoon is fitted as a snaffle and the curb sits just below it. Always check inside the mouth to make sure the curb is well clear of the tushes. If it is very close both bits may need to be raised a hole. The curb chain must lie flat and be placed down on to the hook to avoid it turning over.

COMPETITION RULES

Some bits and items of tack are not permitted for certain competitions. Unaffiliated and Pony Club tend to follow affiliated rules. It is important to check you are using the correct equipment before arriving at the competition.

SADDLES

The saddle must be a good fit in order for the horse to perform well. The horse will tolerate a lot, but if pain is not removed he will become more sore and unable to produce his best. Often the early signs are not recognized or are overlooked and the problem will become worse and performance will suffer. In many cases it leads to napping or refusing to jump. It is important to check regularly the fit of your saddle and take immediate action when required.

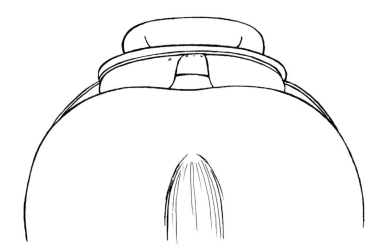

Fitting

- When trying a new or secondhand saddle always examine thoroughly before trying on the horse.
- Check the tree is not damaged.
- Place the saddle on a saddle horse to check it sits evenly.
- Turn upside down and check that the panels are stuffed evenly.
- Thoroughly examine the condition, check stitching, girth straps, stirrup bars, D rings and the condition of the leather.
- The saddle must be tried on the horse without a numnah or pad.
- Put the saddle on and fasten the girth.
- Stand back and examine how the saddle is sitting. It must be level from front to back. Tipping forwards or backwards will affect the rider's balance and apply uneven pressure on the back.
- View the saddle from behind. Stand high enough to check for daylight from front to back. It must also sit level from side to side. Uneven stuffing in the saddle or muscle development on the horse will cause it to sit crookedly.
- It must not sit too far back on the loins.
- It must not sit too far forward and interfere with the shoulder action.
- There must be at least four fingers' clearance at the withers.
- It must not squeeze tight at the withers.
- The saddle flaps should lie flat against the shoulder.
- It is important to sit in the saddle and make the same checks. It then must be tried in at least walk and trot to make sure it sits well and doesn't move about too much.

When to check

The stuffing in the saddle will become compressed over time and this will cause pressure in certain areas. It will also drop at the wither but this can be checked by placing your fingers under the pommel. The young horse changes shape as he develops. From the age of three to seven years he may need to have the saddle changed frequently. A horse that is unfit after a holiday will not be the same shape as when hunting or competition fit and a horse recovering from long term lameness or illness may have gained weight or lost muscle.

TEMPORARY MEASURES

It is not practical to change your saddle for all of the above cases. An unfit horse will return to his original shape when fit again. It may be possible to use riser pads to improve the fit of the saddle for a short period of time. When the horse is back to his normal shape the saddle should be re-checked and alterations done if necessary.

Areas to check for all ill-fitting saddles

- When grooming or tacking up spend time running your hands over the saddle area. If the horse reacts in an unusual manner it is likely he is feeling something.
- When a horse comes back into work after time off he may become skin sore in the back or girth area. This will be evident when grooming or touching the skin. He will react to very little pressure. When reacting to firmer pressure it is more likely to be muscle sore. This is usually related to an ill-fitting saddle.
- Check more thoroughly around the withers. Stand up high and check for rubbed hair.
- Check for sensitivity where the rider sits. If the hair is rubbed it is likely the saddle is moving about causing friction.
- If the horse is more sore on one side than the other, the stuffing should be checked. This can also be the result of a rider sitting crookedly.
- Large swellings are usually a sign of pressure.
- Small lumps are often caused by grease in the coat. However if not treated the saddle may rub them.

- Thoroughly check the girth area for lumps, rubs and pain on pressure. When a horse is very fit the saddle will tend to slip back and when going cross-country it is necessary to do the girth up very tight and wear a breastplate. The pressure of the saddle slipping back and the breastplate stopping it can cause large swellings under the girth area. They can be very painful to the touch and also when the front legs are stretched forward. This can be a detrimental to the show jump phase at a three-day event.

TREATMENT

- Find and remove the cause.
- Open wounds must be cleaned, allowed to heal and the skin hardened before the saddle and girth are used again.
- If the area is skin sore it will need a few days until the sensitivity has gone by which time the skin should be hardened.
- If saddle pressure has been untreated for a longer period it may cause soreness in the muscles and this may affect performance. A longer period of rest is required and in some cases veterinary advice sought. The vet may administer anti-inflammatory drugs and suggest physiotherapy.
- The physiotherapist may want to look at the saddle on the horse to identify the areas of pressure. They will treat as necessary and advise on after care and work programme.
- The saddle must be altered to fit the horse before using again, otherwise the problem will repeat itself.

EXERCISE

There are other methods of schooling and keeping the horse fit when he cannot be ridden

- Lunge (a roller can be used with side reins if this doesn't interfere with the problem)
- Lunge over poles or jumps
- Long rein
- Loose school/jump
- Ride and lead
- Horse walker

- Swimming
- Treadmill
- Turnout

STIRRUP LEATHERS

- Must be made of good quality leather and well stitched.
- Buffalo or rawhide are the strongest and suitable for jumping, cross-country, hunting or racing. Buffalo will stretch but can be bought pre-stretched.
- The leathers must be a suitable length and width for the rider and type of saddle. For example, dressage leathers will need to be longer than cross-country leathers.
- The condition of the leathers must be checked at least once a week and prior to competition. Areas that are likely to wear first are at the stitching, frequently used holes and where the stirrup iron sits. Older leathers may stretch and become very thin.
- Repaired leathers are much weaker than new leathers. It is not advisable to use them for hunting, jumping, fast work or competition.

STIRRUP IRONS

- Must be a suitable size for the rider.
- Should be suited to the type of saddle and work.
- All irons must have good grip for the foot.
- Safety irons are suitable for children.
- There are various makes of lightweight irons, suitable for cross-country.
- Some irons are designed to help the rider maintain the correct foot position in the stirrup.

GIRTHS

Synthetic

These are my choice for cross-country and their advantages include:
- Made from soft material, comfortable to the horse and tend not to rub.

- Lightweight.
- Do not get too hot.
- Hard wearing.
- Machine washable.
- Inexpensive.
- Suitable for all disciplines. Available with or without elastic inserts. Can also buy for saddles with long girth straps.

Leather

These are my choice for dressage and show jumping. They are expensive and points to consider include:

- Available in several designs, the most popular being Balding, Atherstone or three fold. These are shaped to prevent girth galls.

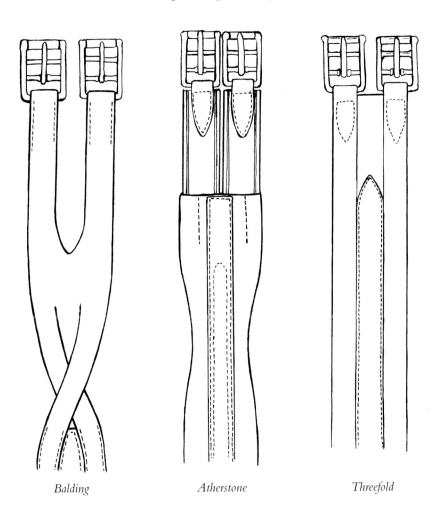

Balding   *Atherstone*   *Threefold*

- Hard wearing if well looked after.
- Must be cleaned daily and stitching well maintained. It is not advisable to use older repaired girths for hunting, jumping and cross-country.
- Available with or without elastic inserts.
- Available with loops to thread the overgirth through.
- Look very smart for competition.

Webbing

Two separate girths that are attached to the girth straps which makes them safer if a strap breaks. They are used in racing and cross-country. The pros and cons include:

- Lightweight.
- Easy to wash.
- Can cause girth galls.

Manmade

There are different types on the market and they are my choice for everyday use. The leather lookalike and webbing ones covered in a plastic material look quite smart. Points to consider include:

- Easy to clean.
- Inexpensive.
- Will not last as long as leather and not as easy to repair.

Girth sleeve

The pros and cons of a girth sleeve include:

- Used to prevent girth galls or to keep a girth clean.
- Useful when a horse is coming back in to work after time off and for horses that are prone to girth galls.
- Available in sheepskin or synthetic material.
- Will cause the horse to sweat more.
- Can be bulky and difficult to fit with a martingale or breastplate.

Stud guard

These are used for show jumping and cross-country to prevent the horse from studding himself with the front shoes.

- Available as an all-in-one girth or a separate attachment that is fitted onto the girth.

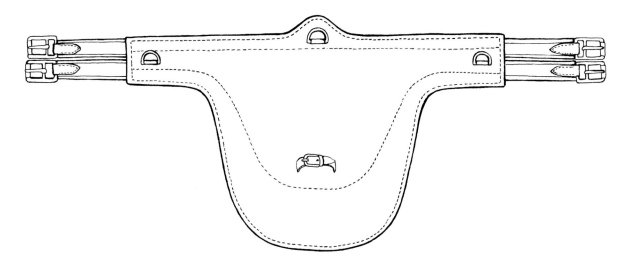

Overgirth

These are used primarily for racing and cross-country and can also be used for show jumping.

- Gives extra security in the event of a broken girth.
- Prevents the saddle bouncing up and down on the horse's back when the rider is in forward position.
- It is important that the overgirth is fitted correctly otherwise girth galls can result.

FITTING

The correct method of fitting overgirths is as follows:
- The saddle is fitted and the girth done up.
- The rider mounts and tightens the girth. Has a walk and trot, re-checks the girth is tight.
- Standing on the near side, pass the overgirth over the saddle – buckle first.

- Go to the other side. Lay the overgirth flat over the girth. If possible passing through the loop of the numnah.
- Go back to the other side and repeat. The buckle and bulky part of the overgirth must not be under the rider's seat or leg.
- Thread through the martingale or breastplate loop. If neither is worn the girth must have loops to pass the overgirth through and secure in place, otherwise it is likely to slip back. Electrical tape can be used as a last resort.
- The overgirth is then tightened.
- Have a final check that both sides are in the correct place.
- Place into keepers.
- A common fault is to tighten the overgirth before the girth is tight. To avoid this, the overgirth can be tightened at the start of the cross-country. This is not advisable if the horse is very excitable as this can prove difficult and risk someone being kicked.

NUMNAHS

- Used to provide comfort and protection to the horse's back.
- Helps to keep the saddle clean.
- Available in various shapes, sizes and materials.

Dressage

White dressage squares are more commonly used. These are longer and straighter cut in the saddle flap than a general purpose or jumping numnah.
- Shaped numnahs can be used but must be designed to fit the saddle.
- They look smart and show the horse off well.
- If the horse is weak in the loin area a larger pad may help to disguise this.
- Must have suitable straps to secure.

Show jumping

A lightweight numnah or square can be used. It must be:
- Forward cut to fit the saddle.
- Have suitable straps to secure.

Cross-country

A numnah or square can be used. The numnah is more suitable at higher level or in hot conditions. The square covers more of the body causing the horse to sweat more. It is important when cooling at a three-day event to fold the square back and apply water underneath.

- Must be lightweight.
- Must be well secured at the girth straps.
- Dark colours are more practical and wash better.

Hunting

The comfort to the horse is most important and thicker numnahs will provide more padding to the back. Sheepskin and cotton absorb sweat well.

Saddle pads

These have the following advantages:

- They help prevent sore backs.
- They can improve the fit of the saddle (as a temporary measure).
- They improve the balance of the saddle, if it is causing the rider to tip forwards or backwards. A riser pad will raise either the front or the back. This must not change the fit of the saddle.
- They are available in a range of shapes, sizes and materials.

CARE OF SADDLERY

Saddle soap

This comes either as a bar or in a tub and is suitable for everyday cleaning of used, well conditioned leather. Good quality saddle soap will soak in well leaving tack soft, supple and shiny and should not create a film on top leaving the leather feeling sticky. I would always recommend using a good quality brand.

Saddle soap spray

This has the same uses as bar saddle soap but is quicker to apply. However it is more difficult to get the desired amount, therefore the leather often becomes too sticky. It can be wasteful but is useful for a quick clean.

Oil

Oil is used on new leather and badly conditioned and dry leather as well as leather that has got wet. It is also useful for leather that has been stored.

- The leather must be cleaned before oiling.
- Apply with a small brush, then massage into the leather with your fingers.
- The leather may become dull in appearance when the oil has soaked in. Apply saddle soap to restore the shine.
- You may need to repeat treatment for a few days until the leather becomes supple.
- Never oil the upper side of a saddle as it will stain breeches.
- Recommended product – Neat's foot oil.

Leather dressing/conditioner

There are various products available on the market which come in liquid and cream form. Points to remember include:

- Used to feed and restore leather.
- The leather must be clean.
- Has the same uses as oil.
- Can be used weekly to give extra condition and protection to leather.
- Recommended products – Kiefer Beeswax leather oil, Ko'choline (may stain), Leather Therapy Restorer and Conditioner, Lincoln Leather Dressing.

Bridle – daily clean

Ideally your bridle should be cleaned after each use. You will need a clean bucket with warm water, two sponges and saddle soap. The method is as follows:

- Wash the bit in warm water.
- Use a damp sponge to remove grease, dirt and mud from both sides of the leather. Frequently clean the sponge, squeeze out well to prevent the leather becoming too wet.

- Use a second sponge to apply saddle soap. This must be thoroughly squeezed out. If it is too wet it will create a foam and not soak into the leather.
- If more moisture is needed to apply the soap, add to the saddle soap rather than the sponge.
- Check the buckles and stitching.
- Replace all straps into keepers.
- Tie the reins into the throatlash and fasten up the noseband.

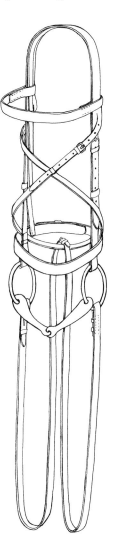

A bridle tied up neatly after cleaning

Bridle – thorough clean

This should be done pre-competition or at least once a week using the following procedure:

- Take the bridle to pieces. Make a note of what holes the cheek pieces and noseband are on.
- Put the bits into hot water.
- Wash each piece of leather separately with a damp sponge. A plastic pan scrub can be used to remove stubborn dirt and grease.
- Check each buckle, billet and all stitching.
- Treat the leather accordingly with soap, oil or leather conditioner.
- Clean out the holes with a match stick.
- Thoroughly wash the bits, using the pan scrub to remove stains from the mouth piece.
- Put the bridle back together.
- Wipe over with saddle soap if looking dull.
- Put all straps in keepers and tie the bridle up.

Martingales and breastplates

These should be wiped over and soaped after each use and must be taken apart, checked and thoroughly cleaned pre-competition.

- Leather to be treated as necessary.
- Extra attention should be paid to the strap that goes to the girth. This is often exposed to more water, especially if used for hunting or cross-country. It may be necessary to oil or treat with leather conditioner more frequently.

- Elasticated breastplates will need scrubbing with a stiff brush and hot water. It is advisable to use a dark colour for competition as they do become very stained.

Cleaning the saddle

The saddle doesn't need cleaning every day unless it is being used in muddy or wet conditions but it should be wiped over at least every third day. It must be stripped and thoroughly cleaned pre-competition or once a week. To do this:

- Have two buckets of warm water.
- Remove leathers and girth.
- Remove irons from leathers and place in bucket of water.
- Wipe over leathers and girth (if leather).
- Wash all parts of saddle with a damp sponge.
- If the saddle has any areas of suede these should not be washed. Allow to dry and clean with a stiff brush.
- All stitching must be thoroughly checked. Special attention must be paid to the stirrup leathers and the girth straps. For example the girth straps may need oiling or treating with saddle soap.
- Treat leather accordingly. Different parts of the saddle may need treating with different products.
- The girth and leathers should be treated as necessary.
- Wash and dry the irons.
- Replace the leather. Pre-competition, the leathers should be at the correct length.
- The girth should lie over the saddle, and through the irons, not attached to the girth straps.
- Apply a saddle cover or place a towel over the saddle to prevent it becoming dusty. Make sure the flaps are lying flat when put on the saddle rack.

New tack

Equipment should be tried on the horse before applying oil and the leather treated before use. It should then be cleaned and oiled after each use until the leather is supple and user friendly.

- Equipment must be well worn in before using in competition.

- Extra holes should be available to lengthen and shorten.
- Holes should be punched when the equipment is off the horse. Mark the leather at the appropriate place, adjust the punch to the correct size hole. The hole must be made in the centre of the leather piece.
- When a pair of holes is needed, for example on stirrup leathers, it is essential to make them even. Make the hole in the first leather. Lay the leather over the top of the second leather, ensuring all the holes are lined up. Mark with a pen, through the new holes onto the under leather. Punch the holes in the marked spots.
- Avoid making holes too close to each other as this weakens the leather.

Metal work

Brass and stainless steel can be polished to improve turnout for competition, this includes brass buckles on bridles and leather headcollars, stirrup irons and trot up chains.

- The metal work should be cleaned first.
- Vinegar can be used to remove stains.
- Apply the polish using a soft, dry cloth to shine.
- The leather around the brass may become dull. Wipe over with saddle soap.
- Recommended products – Silvo, Brasso, Duraglit.

Storing tack

All tack must be thoroughly cleaned before storing and any repairs made. Always store in a dry, damp-proof area remembering that tack not in use will often become mouldy. When storing in a box it will help to wrap the leather in newspaper. To maintain condition it will be necessary to treat with leather conditioner or else the tack will become dry and stiff.

LEG PROTECTION

Because of the unnatural demands and environment we subject horses to it is often necessary to use boots or bandages to protect their legs from injury.

Common sites of
injury

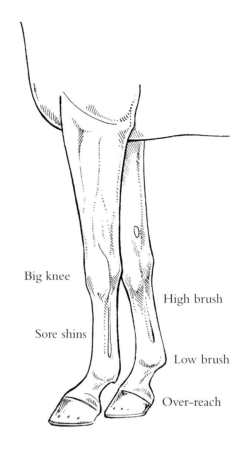

Big knee

High brush

Sore shins

Low brush

Over-reach

However, the legs are not designed to be wrapped up and we can cause more damage by trying to protect them and therefore it is important to choose the most suitable boot or bandage for individual needs. They must then be fitted correctly.

BOOTS

These protect against self-inflicted injuries and knocks. Listed below are the different boots and their uses.

Brushing

The front or hind leg knocks or brushes against the opposite leg, usually making contact at the fetlock. It can cause bruising and swelling to the area. This is caused by a fault in conformation or action, poor foot balance or shoeing, the demands of work (lungeing, riding on small circles and tight turns) or lack of co-ordination (tired, weak or young horses).

Observe your horse when walking and trotting in hand to see how close his legs are when moving. When riding it can often be heard or felt if the horse knocks himself.

Over-reach

The hind foot strikes into the foreleg, usually at the heel area but it can happen higher up. This can be more serious if the tendon is damaged. It is most likely to occur when galloping and jumping, the horse is tired or weak, when riding in deep or heavy terrain, landing steep over a jump or when the horse is fresh when being ridden, lunged or turned out in the field.

Speedy cut

The hind or front foot cuts into the opposite leg below the knee or hock and this happens during fast work and is usually related to the horse's action.

Tread

The horse treads on himself with the opposite foot, causing cuts or bruising to the coronet band or pastern area. This is caused by his action, poor shoeing, freshness when ridden, lunged or loose or when travelling.

Knocks

These can affect any part of the leg but usually appear from the knee and hock downwards. Amongst the causes are the demands of work (such as hitting fences when jumping), falls, travelling or rolling or getting cast in the stable.

CHOOSING THE CORRECT BOOT

There are many boots available, designed to protect against all types of injuries. Before choosing a boot for your horse, consider its purpose. Observe your horse in action. Examine the legs for signs of injury after work.

Work boots

Used for hacking, dressage, jumping, fast work, lungeing, loose schooling/
jumping, long reining.

BRUSHING BOOT

- Made from synthetic material. Reinforced on the inside to provide extra
  protection. Can be lined with foam or sheepskin to prevent rubbing.
- Protects from below the knee and hock to the fetlock.
- Velcro fastening (double straps provide extra security).
- Quick and easy to fit.
- Machine washable.
- Hard wearing.
- Velcro must be kept clean.

OVER-REACH BOOT

- Worn in addition to the brushing boot when the horse is very fresh.
- More likely to over reach when lungeing or loose jumping.
- May prevent bar shoes being pulled off. Advisable to wear in the field.
- Synthetic material with Velcro fastening are quick and easy for everyday
  use.

Competition boots

DRESSAGE

- The horse is not permitted to wear boots or bandages in the dressage
  arena
- Brushing boots are suitable for working in.
- White boots are often used to show the horse off more and look very
  smart.
- Polo wraps are also popular (will be discussed with bandages).

SHOW JUMPING BOOTS

It is important to protect the horse from self-inflicted injury but as important
not to protect too much of the leg so that he becomes insensitive to touching
a pole.

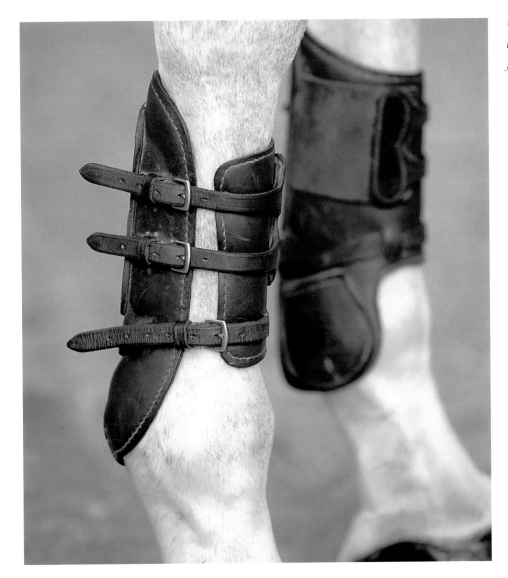

FRONT LEGS

OPEN-FRONTED BOOT

- Protects the back of the leg from below the knee to the tendon, leaving the front of the leg exposed.
- Protects the horse from striking into the tendon.
- Made from leather or synthetic materials.

BRUSHING BOOT

- Offers more protection than open-fronted boots.
- Worn by very careful jumpers or young, green horses.

OVER-REACH BOOTS

- Should be worn if the horse has a tendency to over reach or pull shoes off.
- Rubber is less bulky than synthetic materials.
- Velcro fastenings are easy to fit.
- Petal boots do not turn inside out. Individual petals can be replaced if the boot becomes damaged.

HIND LEGS

Unless the horse brushes it is not necessary to wear boots behind.

FETLOCK BOOTS

- Cover the fetlock joint only.
- Made from leather or synthetic materials.
- Can buy matching sets with open-fronted boots.

BRUSHING BOOT

- Can be worn to offer more protection.

SPEADY CUT BOOTS

- Designed as a cross-country boot, protecting higher and lower than the brushing boot.
- More sturdy than brushing boots, made from leather or synthetic materials.
- In my experience some horses are more careful with the hind leg when wearing these boots.
- When first put on, the horse may hold the leg out and walk off with a very 'snatchy hock' action. This may be why they jump cleaner with the hind leg
- If used too often the effect will wear off. The horse can be worked in and practise jumped without them. The boots should be put on just before the horse goes into the ring.

CROSS-COUNTRY
FRONT
TENDON BOOTS

- Made from synthetic materials.
- Similar shape to a brushing boot. Has extra protection down the back of

the leg. This must be soft and mould to the tendon. Some have a very rigid insert which can squeeze the tendon and cause damage.

- Must be lightweight and not hold water.
- Create as little heat as possible.
- Secure wide straps. Velcro fastening must be kept clean and always secured with tape. Double Velcro is ideal.
- Quick and easy to apply.

LEATHER BOOTS
- Sturdy, hard wearing.
- Offer ample protection.
- More difficult to fit than tendon boots and often slip down.
- Straps can be done too tight causing pressure points on the tendons.
- More difficult to maintain condition.

OVER-REACH BOOTS
- Should always be worn.
- Must be lightweight and not bulky.
- Pull-on rubber ones are the most suitable.
- The bottom of the boot should not come lower than the bulbs of the heel. This is to prevent the horse treading on the boot and causing a fall.
- The boot should be trimmed to size.

HIND
BRUSHING BOOT
- Offers enough protection when competing at lower levels.
- Must be in good condition with secure straps.
- Must fit well.
- Tape must be used to secure straps.

SPEEDY CUT
- Made from leather or synthetic materials.
- More suitable for higher levels or for horses prone to speedy cut injuries.
- Must fit well and not slip down.
- Good secure fastening. Leather buckles must be well cared for and

checked before each use. They are more difficult to fit and can be time-consuming.

- Velcro fastenings are much quicker and easier to fit. Must be secured with tape.

Guidelines for fitting boots

- The boot must be the correct length. It should fit around the leg meeting easily in all places, allowing the straps to fasten easily.
- New leather boots should not fasten on the last hole. The leather will stretch and the boot become too big.
- The straps should always fasten on the outside of the leg.
- The majority of straps fasten from the front of the leg to the back. This reduces the risk of creating uneven pressure on the flexor tendons when the straps are secured.
- Double Velcro should be fastened with the under strap from front to back. The upper strap is there to secure this.
- The boot should be placed on the leg slightly higher than intended. It is then moved down into place.
- Secure the central strap first.
- Check the boot is sitting correctly. Secure the remaining straps, starting with the lowest and working up the leg. This will prevent the boot from slipping if the horse moves his leg.
- The straps must be firm, without being tight. The boot should look snug on the leg.
- It is difficult to do plain straps too tight. Elasticated inserts are often over done.
- The boot should not move when pushed down.
- The joints must not be restricted in any way.
- The horse should not be showing signs of discomfort.
- All straps must be secured in keepers.
- Tape must be used with Velcro straps when going cross-country. It must be applied from the front to the back of the leg, taking care not to pull unevenly. It is not used to tighten a strap, only to secure.
- If the horse will not stand still to be booted up it is advisable to have assistance. The opposite foreleg can be held, or for a hind leg, the front leg on the same side.

FITTING OVER-REACH BOOTS

Pull-on over-reach boots are easier to apply when wet. Stand facing the horse's tail, lift up the foot and place between your legs (as the farrier does when shoeing). The boot is turned inside out and placed onto the foot upside down. It is then pulled from one side of the heel to the other. Place the horse's foot on the ground and turn the boot the correct way out.

BOOT INJURIES

More injuries are caused by boots than most people realize. As I mentioned earlier, the leg was not designed to wear a boot.

Boot rubs

There are a number of reasons for these including boots of an incorrect size or shape, being too tight or too loose, worn for long periods of time, mud or debris working its way into the boot (this is why boots are rarely worn for hunting). Another cause is if they are made from poor quality material, causing excess sweating or holding water.

Strap injuries

Over tightening the straps can cause uneven pressure on the tendon, often resulting in bruising. This is more likely to occur from thin straps, often found in leather boots. Elasticated straps give a little providing more comfort, however, they are frequently done up too tightly causing pressure points. The broader the strap the more even the pressure is distributed and fewer, larger straps are safer.

Preventing problems
* Always use correct size and type of boot.
* Time and care should be taken when fitting.
* When using a new or unfamiliar boot it is advisable to seek advice on fit.
* Talcum powder can be sprinkled into the boot to help prevent rubbing.
* Tubi grip is often used under cross-country boots at three-day events to

prevent rubbing. This will cause the leg to heat up and is debateable whether it is worth it.

- Do not use boots if they are not needed.

BANDAGES

Reasons for bandaging

- For protection.
- For warmth.
- To prevent the legs 'filling' (ie swelling).
- To hold a dressing or poultice in place.
- To dry the legs.
- To keep the legs clean.

Types of bandage

EXERCISE BANDAGE

- Used to protect the leg when working.

- Covers the same area as a brushing boot.
- Must be applied over padding, for example Fibregee or Gamgee.
- Very difficult and time consuming to apply well and can cause injury to the leg when put on badly.
- Rarely used.

POLO WRAPS

- Thick felt bandages used for exercise.
- Non-stretch which reduces the risk of applying too tightly.
- Will slip down if put on too loosely. Not suitable for fast work or jumping.
- Soft material reduces the risk of rubbing. Ideal for horses that are prone to boot rubs.
- Machine washable.
- Time consuming.

STABLE BANDAGE

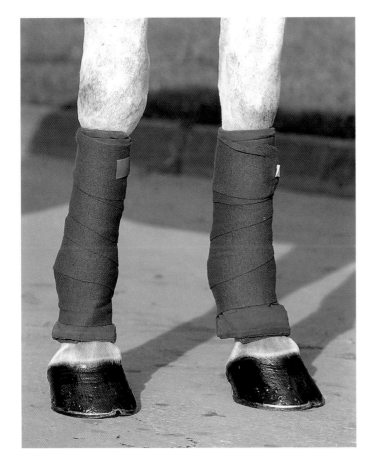

Stable bandage with cotton under wraps

- Prevents the legs 'filling'.
- Provides warmth.
- Keeps the legs clean prior to competition.
- Acts as protection for horses that roll or are prone to getting cast. Advisable to use when stabling at competitions in small temporary stables.
- Dries the legs off after washing in cold weather.
- The bandage should always be applied over padding. It should cover from below the knee and hock joint to below the fetlock joint.
- Slightly elasticated bandages are easier to apply and stay in place.

TRAVEL BANDAGE
- Used to protect the legs during transportation.
- The same type of bandage as the stable bandage.
- The bandage covers the same area as a stable bandage but the padding must come lower to give protection to the heels.

SURGICAL BANDAGES
- Used to secure poultices and dressings.
- Equiwrap or Vetwrap is the easiest and most effective. The whole bandage is often not needed. The required amount can be cut and the remaining wrapped up and saved.
- Care must be taken not to apply too tightly - the leg is likely to swell around the injury.
- A stable bandage can be applied over to add protection to the wound and prevent the leg from 'filling'.
- The opposite leg should be bandaged for support as this may 'fill' because it is taking more weight than the injured leg.

KNEE AND HOCK BANDAGES
- Rarely used as they are difficult to apply and secure.
- Elasticated exercise bandage or surgical are the most effective.
- A figure of eight method of bandaging is used to allow the horse freedom to move the joint.
- Care must be taken to not bandage over the pisiform bone at the back of the knee. A pressure sore will develop, often causing more problems than the original injury.

- A stable bandage should always accompany the knee or hock bandage.

FOOT POULTICE

- Use a surgical, elastic or Equiplast to secure a foot poultice.
- The foot must be dry and clean.
- The bandage is applied in a figure of eight, covering the heels.
- Tape should be used to secure.
- It is advisable to cover with a poultice boot or thick plastic bag.

A poultice boot

TAIL BANDAGE

- Used to protect the tail when travelling or improve the appearance.
- Elastic bandage is ideal.
- Care must be taken not to apply too tight. It should never be left on over night.

A well applied tail bandage

Under-bandage protection

When bandaging the legs with elasticated bandages it is always advisable to use under padding. This will prevent the bandage rubbing and reduce the risk of applying too tight.

FIBRE GEE

- Easy to apply.
- Machine washable (never wash with Velcro as it sticks to it).
- Hard wearing.
- Bedding sticks to it. Not ideal for horses bedded on shavings.

GAMGEE

- Easy to apply. Moulds to the leg more than Fibre gee.
- Can be cut to required size.
- More useful for surgical, knee and hock bandages.
- Does not last a long time.

COTTON WRAPS

- Available in various lengths and thicknesses.
- Can be bulky and more difficult to apply.
- Machine washable.
- Hard wearing.
- Bedding does not stick to them. Ideal for every day use.

Rules for bandaging

- Always bandage over padding.
- The bandage must be rolled up firmly the correct way by folding the Velcro back together and rolling in on itself.
- The under padding must be applied snugly to the leg if the bandage is to be firm enough.

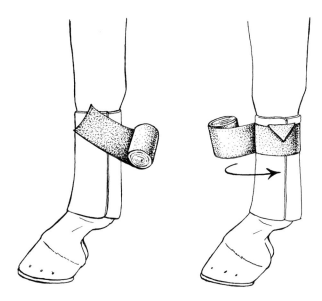

Always bandage over padding   *The bandage must always be applied from front to back*

- Start midway down the leg. Always bandage from the front of the leg to the back. This prevents pressure being applied on the flexor tendons.
- Keep the pressure constant throughout. Each wrap should be even, working down the leg first, covering half the previous wrap. Come back up the leg in the same way.
- Ideally the bandage should finish below the knee, no more than three quarters way down.
- Tapes must be tied on the outside. If they are at the front or back of the leg they may cause pressure to the tendons. There is a risk of them coming undone when on the inside as the opposite leg may interfere. Velcro is safer than tapes.
- The bandage must not be so tight that a finger cannot slide down it.
- It must be firm enough that it does not slide down when pushed.

STUDS

Studs are used to provide extra grip to the shoes, primarily when working on grass. They are occasionally used on a surface. Road studs can also be fitted to prevent slipping when hacking out.

When to use
Without studs the horse is at great risk of slipping and losing confidence in his work. Careful consideration must be taken when selecting appropriate studs. In my opinion competing without studs is not a wise option.

ADVANTAGES
- Prevents the horse from slipping or falling over.
- Gives the horse more confidence when jumping, therefore improves performance.
- Enables you to ride a more accurate dressage test as the horse will not slip on the turns and circles.
- Encourages the rider to ride more positively as you are not worried about the horse slipping.

DISADVANTAGES

- Alters the balance of the foot which will hit the ground at a different angle. This can cause twisting and jarring to the leg.
- It is safer to use two studs in each shoe, placed evenly at each heel. This will help to balance the foot fall. The danger of using a stud on the inside is that the horse may strike into himself. Horses that move very close must only ever wear a small road stud on the inside.
- If one stud is used, this is placed on the outside heel. This is not advisable on hard ground as it will cause severe twisting to the joint.
- Using studs on hard ground may also cause the horse to shorten his stride. When studs are too big or uneven it may also cause the stride to become unlevel.

Studs should not only be used in competition. If the horse is trained without them and slips into a jump, it will not be sufficient to put the studs in at the competition and expect him to regain his confidence. The horse must go to the competition confident so that maximum effort can be asked of him. I would advise using studs for all show jumping on grass and cross-country training.

Types of stud

Studs come in various shapes and sizes. The general rule is the wetter the ground, the bigger the stud. Consideration must also be taken into the length of grass and type of soil and also of the horse's action and way of going. Always try to put as small a stud as possible in the front shoes. The weight on the forehand is much greater, therefore more risk of strain to the fore legs

SMALL ROAD

Used on hard ground or as the inside stud for horses that move very close.

LARGE ROAD

Used as a pair in front, ideal for hard or 'good going'. This is my choice for the front shoes whenever possible. Also suitable for the inside hind shoe, accompanied by a larger outside stud if the ground is slippery.

SMALL POINTS

Useful for 'good going' or when the grass is longer and the road stud does not cut through. Not advisable as an inside stud as can cause serious injury to the opposite leg.

LARGE STUDS

Available in various shapes and sizes. Must only be used in wet ground. When the going is soft the stud will go in easily and there is less chance of jarring. Having had experience of injury, I am very cautious of putting large studs on the inside. In very wet conditions I prefer to use the large road stud on the inside and a big stud on the outside.

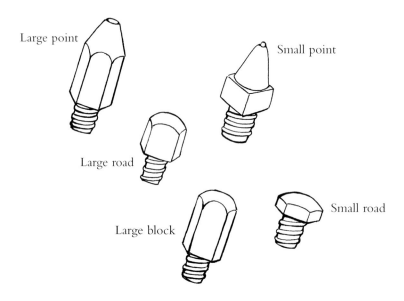

Large point

Small point

Large road

Large block

Small road

TYPES OF GROUND

It is often thought studs are only needed in wet going but this is not so and often wet ground does not cause the horse to slip as the hoof 'cuts' into the ground. In my experience it is much worse to have hard ground with very little covering, or with long grass. It can become very slippery when hard ground has a small amount of rain; this tends to sit on the surface rather than soaking in causing it to become very 'greasy'. At a competition it is often necessary to change studs throughout the day or for different disciplines.

Care of stud holes

You must inform your farrier if you want shoes with stud holes and you will need the following equipment:

- Bradal or nail for cleaning holes
- Tap
- Spanner
- Cotton wool/sponge for plugging holes
- Baby oil
- WD40

To fit the studs:

- Remove dirt and stones from the feet and holes.
- Spray the hole with WD40.
- Use the tap to clean the threads. Care must be taken not to cross the threads. The tap must turn easily, if it has to be forced it is likely not to be in correctly. If the threads are crossed the stud cannot be secured in the hole. The less the tap is used the longer the holes will last. It will often not be necessary to use the tap but you will still have to clean the hole, spray and try the stud.
- The stud is then tightened using the spanner.
- Studs must always be removed after use.
- The holes can be plugged using sponge or cotton wool soaked in baby oil.

Dirt and stones are removed from the hole

The threads are cleaned by carefully using the tap

The spanner is used to tighten the stud

Care of studs

Studs should be cleaned after use, stored in a dry container, sprayed with WD40 or covered with oil to prevent rusting. Always carry spare studs of each set as they are frequently lost.

CHAPTER 8
Travelling

One of the most important aspects of looking after the competition horse is the care whilst travelling. Transporting, whether it be by road, air or sea causes stress to all horses to varying degrees. The fact that the horse is confined to a small space, often with poor air circulation predisposes him to problems related to the circulatory, respiratory and digestive systems. Being in an unnatural environment will also lead to mental stress. Unlike us they don't share the same comforts when travelling. Try standing in the back of a horsebox when it is moving and you will soon discover that it is hard work to keep your balance and would be extremely tiring on a long journey. Our aim must be to reduce the risk of physical and mental stress by providing the best possible comfort and environment for our horse. It is also essential that we learn to recognize the signs of stress as early as possible. Failure to do so may affect the performance of the horse and lead to illness. During longer journeys this can become very serious and develop into shipping fever which can be fatal.

MAINTENANCE OF THE HORSEBOX

Tax and insurance
As with any vehicle these must be kept up to date. Make a reminder of when they are due in your competition diary. This will give you time to renew well in advance and not interrupt any competition plans.

Test

Horseboxes have to be tested annually. It is advisable to have a reputable mechanic service the vehicle before testing. It is ideal for this to take place during a quiet period or during the 'off season'. It can prove very inconvenient if major work has to be done during the season and competitions are missed!

Breakdown cover

It is strongly recommended that you are covered for emergency roadside assistance. It can be an extremely daunting experience breaking down on a busy road or motorway with horses on board. Being towed home or finding alternative transport can prove very costly. Details of your cover must be kept in the vehicle and filed at home where they can be easily found in an emergency.

FITTINGS

Floors

These must be non-slip as the horse will move about a lot. The majority of floors are wood covered in rubber. This must lie flat and be well secured to the material underneath. If it becomes loose it will move about and become dangerous, nails may also start to protrude which the horse could tread on. Wooden floors are acceptable; they are much safer if they have a form of grip. The advantage of wooden floors is that it is easier to recognize when the wood is rotting and needs replacing. Covering with rubber prevents this and after time the wood will start to rot but may go unnoticed. Older horseboxes must have the rubber lifted from time to time to check the condition. Thorough cleaning and allowing the floor to dry out will prolong this happening.

Partitions

These come in many designs and the simplest is a single metal bar dividing each section. This offers little protection to the horse. The ideal is a metal frame with a strong wooden board to the floor or wood half way down and rubber to the floor. This provides the horse with something to lean on if balance is lost. It also prevents him from kicking or stepping on the horse next to him. Many horses use the partition as support and will travel with their full weight on it. Sponge type padding will offer some protection. It is quite common to see sore hips on horses that don't travel well and have not been provided with protection. All partitions must be adjustable as each horse may vary in the size of space they find easier to balance in during travel. They must open and close freely and have a means of tying back if they are likely to swing when a horse is being loaded or unloaded.

Headboards

They prevent the horses making contact with each other. They can be a dangerous fitting if incorrectly designed and if made too small the horse will attempt to get his head under or over them and the headcollar can then get caught and cause panic. They must be a suitable size that the horse is not tempted to do this. They must be easily removed, adjustable and free from protruding fastenings.

Tie rings

Each travelling space must be provided with a tie ring. This must be a suitable size and attached firmly to the bodywork. It is extremely unsafe to attempt to tie the horse to any other fitting such as the bars on the windows. The tie ring should not be placed too high. Travelling with the head in a raised position can cause respiratory disorders. For safety, string can be attached to each ring. Alternately I prefer each ring to be fitted with a quick release rubber-covered chain. This should be a suitable length that the horse has movement from side to side and can freely eat his haynet. It should not allow for him to turn his head too much or attempt to reach the horse next to him. I prefer to have the quick release clip attached to the ring rather than the headcollar. I have experienced horses that have got themselves stuck in certain positions. They are liable to panic and trying to get to the head to release the tie can prove difficult and often dangerous. It is much safer to release the horse from the ring. The tie ring can also double up as a haynet ring; again haynets must not be attached to other less secure fittings. A separate ring placed slightly higher is the ideal. Some horses become very aggressive being in a confined space close to other horses. In this case I prefer to cross tie them. This requires two rings to attach a rope from either side of the headcollar. This allows the horse to have freedom of the head without being able to get to the horses at either side of him.

Windows

The more fresh air available when travelling, the less chance of illness. Windows should open and close freely, ideally by sliding up and down. They must be protected by bars on the inside.

Ventilation

If the horsebox doesn't have windows it is essential it has other means of ventilation. Without it the air will quickly become stale and lead to respiratory problems. Modern horseboxes are equipped with skylights, these being useful when the vehicle is stationary or in hot weather. In cold weather the horse should be well rugged to keep warm rather than closing the ventilation which will prevent the circulation of fresh air.

Ramp

This must be strong, non-slip and user-friendly. The most common being made of wood covered with rubber. Wooden slats are added to give extra grip. These do wear quickly on heavily used ramps but are easy to replace. Other variations include metal which needs to be covered as it can be slippery and very noisy which may unnerve the horse. Coconut matting or carpet can be used as covering; they are cheaper but not as easy to keep clean. As with the floor regular checks must be made on the condition of the ramp. After use it should be thoroughly swept and left open to dry. The springs on the ramp should be well maintained making it easy and safe to put up and down. Some horseboxes are fitted with hydraulic ramps; obviously they have their advantages but can breakdown causing inconvenience and in rare cases become dangerous.

Lockers

Modern horseboxes are fitted with lockers that can be used for storing feed and equipment. The internal lockers often run in front of the horses. Checks must be made to ensure the locks are in good condition and not likely to open during travelling. External lockers should have strong, well maintained doors. It is advisable that they lock if intended to carry expensive equipment. The advantages of having external lockers are that it leaves more space to carry horses, it is easier to obtain equipment and quicker to get horses ready outside. It does however restrict tying up space outside the lorry and is not so convenient in bad weather.

Rug racks

These usually run along the length of the lorry above the hindquarters. Ideal for storing rugs, numnahs and bandages, they can be open-topped or totally enclosed. Care must be taken when packing equipment onto the open topped as it may fall off during the journey if items are not folded and pressed flat. The closed ones are more secure but not as easy to get in to.

Lights

Windows and skylights will provide ample light throughout the day. By law the horsebox must have internal lighting. All lights should be covered for safety and kept dry and clean. It is also advisable to have a light that shines onto the ramp which will help when loading and unloading in the dark.

External tie rings

These will run along either one or both sides of the horsebox. Vary them in height so that some are low enough to allow the horse to graze. Care must be taken not to tie the horse too long as it is easy to get a leg over the rope. Higher rings are much safer and the horses usually stand happily with a haynet. The disadvantage of tying outside is damage can be done to the bodywork by biting or kicking. To avoid this a protective cover can be attached to the side of the lorry with holes for the tie rings. This is expensive but less so than a re-spray.

179

Water tanks

These are built in to most modern horseboxes. It is much more convenient than carrying water containers. Some are fitted with an external tap others have a hosepipe, which is ideal for washing off. The water tank should be labelled to avoid the mistake of filling with diesel as this would be irreparable. The tank should be drained during the winter as freezing weather may cause the tank to burst.

TRAILERS

Trailers are a more popular form of transport for the one horse owner. To provide a comfortable journey it is necessary to have a suitable towing vehicle such as a four-wheel drive and you should check the current regulations about suitable vehicles to ensure that you are within the law.

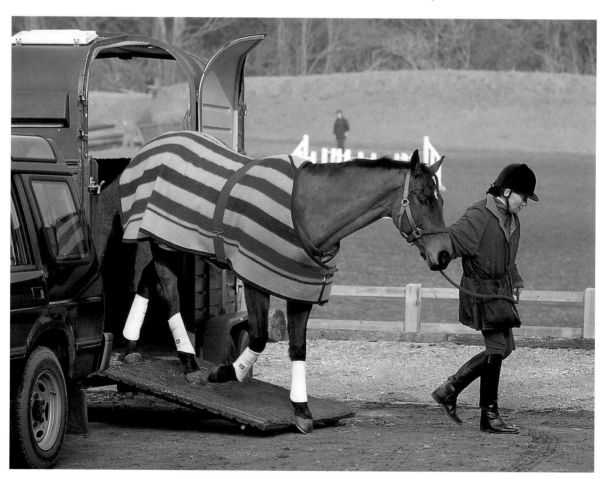

The following factors need to be taken into account:

- Maintenance of bodywork, interior and exterior fittings should be as previously discussed. It is also essential that the towing equipment is regularly checked.

- The towing hitch must be in excellent condition. The towing vehicle must match this in height and size.

- The electrical fittings for the lights must be checked before each journey. Care must be taken to keep them dry when not in use.

- The jockey wheel must be in good working order.

- It is advisable to have a safety chain in the event of the trailer becoming unhitched. Modern trailers are fitted with an automatic brake.

- Tyres should be checked frequently for wear and correct pressure.

- Half doors should open and close freely giving either option while travelling. Ventilation is important but having all doors open in bad weather may cause a chill.

- The correct number plate should be well fitted and clearly visible on the back of the trailer.

PREPARATION OF HORSEBOX FOR TRAVELLING

- Vehicle must be mechanically in good working order. Prior to long journeys or trips overseas I would advise a thorough service if one has not been carried out recently.

- Check oil and water.

- Check there is sufficient diesel to get to nearest service station on intended route. If leaving early more local petrol stations may be closed. If in doubt it is safer to fill up the day before.

- All fittings must be in good working order.

- Partitions should be fitted for number and size of horses. The table shows the space requirements stated by DEFRA.

ADULT HORSES	0.7 x 2.5m
YOUNG HORSES (6 to 24 MONTHS) (Journey up to 48 hours)	0.6 x 2.0m
YOUNG HORSES (6 to 24 MONTHS) (Journey over 49 hours)	1.2 x 2.0m
PONIES (UNDER 144CM)	0.6 x 1.8m
FOALS (0 to 6 MONTHS)	1.0 x 1.4m

This can be used as a general guideline. You must however observe your horse during travel and recognize how he prefers to stand. Some will balance by spreading the hindlegs very wide; these require a larger space and will often panic if they don't have room to do this. Others will lean against the partition, usually one side only. Providing too much space will cause them to move about from side to side when braking or driving on twisty roads. Bad travellers can be quite alarming and I have witnessed horses fall over in panic. Altering the amount of space they have can often make all the difference.

- Water tanks and containers freshly filled. The horse will need to be offered water during long journeys. Water buckets must be easily accessible.

- Haynets filled. It is not always necessary to travel with a haynet but it does often help to settle the horse.

- When travelling long distances or overseas it will be necessary to feed during the journey. The feeds can be prepared before departure. A suitable manger is required that can be fixed at a comfortable height. Carry carrots and apples as the horse may be reluctant to eat.

- Bedding can be put down and dust-free such as shavings or paper is advisable. The advantage of having bedding is it will encourage the horse to stale. Many horses are reluctant to do so; this can lead to discomfort and inhibit performance. The bedding will also soak up the urine and provide better working conditions. I prefer to put a strip of bedding under the horse to catch the urine and leave the back free where the droppings fall. It is easier to skip out without wasting too much clean bedding. In the case of a mare it needs to be all the way back. The disadvantage of bedding is that it tends to blow about a lot and cause a mess. To avoid this move it well forward when the ramp is dropped.

PREPARATION FOR BAD TRAVELLERS

If your horse doesn't travel well preparations must be made to prevent injury and relieve stress. The partitions should be arranged to suit. It may help to provide more padding as protection if the horse leans or is likely to throw himself about. I have used duvets and pillows to provide more cushioning. Some horses will sit back on their hocks and this can cause rubs on the point of buttock, again I have hung a duvet behind the horse which has helped. I would recommend putting down extra bedding as the risk of the floor becoming slippery will make matters worse.

Try travelling the horse in a different part of the lorry. It may make a difference if he is at the front as this does create a smoother ride. Giving a haynet or even a small feed may help to distract him. It is important he is tied at the correct length and with a quick release rope. If tying to string make sure it is not too thick as it may not break. Bale string at full thickness is not suitable and should be shredded in half. Seriously bad travellers should not be left unattended as they are likely to cause themselves injury.

A bad traveller puts a tremendous amount of stress on himself and even if the signs are not visible the thrashing and leaning will cause considerable discomfort. One horse I had that didn't travel well had to have physiotherapy following a long journey. He would be very sore in his hamstrings as he travelled with his weight on his hindquarters.

PREPARATION OF HORSES

If at all possible avoid travelling horses that are 'off colour'. The added stress of travelling may cause a slight illness to develop into something much more serious.

Short journeys – less than eight hours

For most of us an average drive to a competition takes between two to four hours. Occasionally we might travel further to bigger events. Preparing for shorter journeys takes less planning and becomes routine.

Clothing

When preparing the horse to travel take into consideration the following:

- Weather conditions
- Type of coat and whether or not the horse is clipped
- Type and size of horsebox
- Number of horses travelling
- Length of journey
- How the horse travels

HEADCOLLAR

- Leather or nylon
- Ensure that it is a suitable fit – large enough to fit over the bridle
- Good condition

ROPE

- Strong and in good condition
- Suitable length
- Strong clip – quick release is preferable if using to tie up in horsebox

POLL GUARD

This is optional but recommended for large horses travelling in low-roofed vehicles and also for youngsters or horses which are head shy.

RUGS

It is not unusual for the horse to change temperature frequently during a journey, often to the extent of sweating then cooling down. Choosing the correct rug to travel can be difficult and it may be necessary to change the rug during the journey. The following are the most suitable and popular rugs to use.

SWEAT NET – Useful in very hot weather to give the horse some protection against flies. If worn with another rug on top it allows the horse to cool and the top rug would prevent him getting a chill.

COOLER – More than a sweat rug it will keep the horse warm. It will absorb sweat, allowing the coat to dry and prevent the horse from getting cold as it does so. Available in various thicknesses it is suitable for all year round.

SUMMER SHEET – Suitable for horses that don't sweat when travelling. Ideal in summer to keep the horse clean and to protect from flies.

DAY RUG – Useful for clipped horses or in cold weather. If the horse tends to sweat a cooler or sweat rug can be worn under. The front of the day rug can be quartered back.

SURCINGLE

ELASTIC – These are the most common as they are cheap and easy to apply. They must be fitted tight enough as they can slip back and become a bucking strap, especially on the fit, lean horse.

ROLLERS – More suitable if the rugs slip but less comfortable for the horse as it is similar to having a girth on.

CROSS SURCINGLE – Many rugs are fitted with cross straps. They provide more comfort for the horse and take away the pressure of the roller.

LEG STRAPS - It is not advisable to travel in a rug with leg straps. It can be both difficult and dangerous to get to them if the rug needs to be removed whilst travelling.

TAIL BANDAGES

- Care must be taken not to apply too tight.
- To keep a tail clean it can be plaited down, doubled up and a second bandage applied to secure.
- A tail guard can be applied on top for extra protection. I would advise this for plaited tails or horses that rub their tails.
- Tail bags are available, some attach to the rug others attach to a tail guard. They are very useful for nervous travellers and grey horses to help keep them clean.
- For long journeys I prefer to use a tail guard without the tail bandage. This is more comfortable for the horse. A tail bandage should not be left on for a long period of time.

LEG PROTECTION

BANDAGES – These must be applied over padding, the most suitable of which are either cotton wraps or Fibre gee. The aim is to protect the leg from the knee and hock to the heels, therefore the padding must go lower than that of a stable bandage. Care must be taken to get the tension equal. If it is too loose it will slip and too tight could restrict the circulation or cause bruising to the tendon. During long journeys the legs may fill, extra care must be taken when bandaging and regular checks should be made to ensure the bandages have not become too tight. For this reason I prefer to use leg wraps.

Travel bandages should protect the coronet band and heels

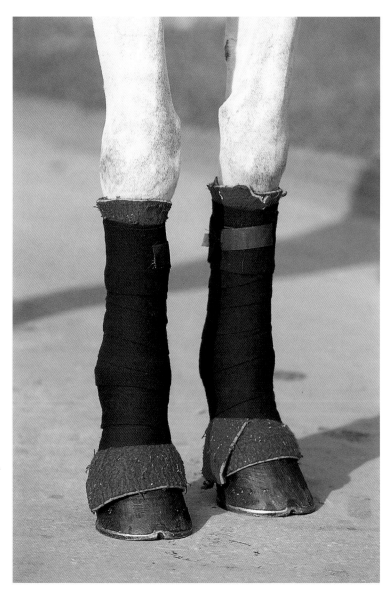

KNEE/HOCK BOOTS – Bandages do not protect the knee and hock. If your horse doesn't travel well it may be necessary to use knee and hock boots as extra protection. It is important that they are fitted correctly. The top strap must be fastened securely to prevent the boots from slipping down. The lower strap is done up very loose to allow flexion of the knee and hock joint. The design of these can cause them to rub especially if on for long periods of time. I would avoid using if at all possible.

LEG WRAPS – These are a much more modern choice of leg protection and are available in various shapes and sizes. They offer protection to the knee and hock down to the heel. Made from soft materials there is less chance of rubbing or injury and Velcro fastenings make them quick and easy to apply.

OVER-REACH BOOTS – These can be used as extra protection to the heels and are advisable if the horse wears bar shoes as there is a risk of treading on the shoe and pulling it off.

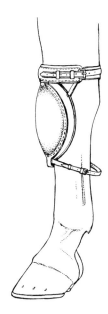

Knee boots can be worn for protection

Travelling tacked up

- Useful when hunting or competing locally especially with young horses that can be difficult first time out.
- The saddle, breastplate and martingale should be put on and fitted correctly.
- The girth should be tight enough to prevent the saddle from slipping back.
- Travelling with the bridle on is optional. When using competition bridles I prefer to them put on when I arrive as the horse will often rub his face and scratch the leather work. Beware of bits with cheeks or long shanks as they can often get caught on things and cause panic. As it is usually a short trip it is wise to tie the horse shorter than usual.
- Suitable work boots can be worn.
- Travel boots can be put over or may not be necessary with good travellers.
- Tail guard should be fitted.
- Appropriate rugs should be put over the tack. The rug must be secured. If the tack is removed to travel home, the surcingle or cross straps must be tightened to prevent the rugs slipping.

Fully equipped for travelling

Avoid feeding large amounts of hard feed immediately before travelling. When leaving for a competition early morning allow half an hour after the horse has finished the feed before loading. Some horses don't mind being groomed and prepared for travel while they eat. Others may be put off their food by this and should be allowed to finish before getting them ready.

If you know your horse is reluctant to stale on the lorry or at the competition try to encourage him to do so before loading. Skipping out and moving the bed may help. Try whistling as this often has the desired effect.

Long journeys / overseas

It is important to plan well ahead for long journeys or travelling abroad. A considerable amount of stress is put on the horse, whether it is by sea, air or a long trip by road. When travelling to a competition, allow sufficient time for recovery before the competition begins.

When travelling abroad it is advisable to go through a reputable shipping company. They will provide you with information on health papers, blood tests, route plans, sailing or flight options, rest periods and suitable stables to rest at during the journey. When sailing there can often be delays due to bad weather. They will advise on how long the delays, options of sailing from a different port and provide a new route plan. If the delay is long they will provide temporary stabling.

Certain countries require your horse to be accompanied by health papers. Your shipping agent or vet will advise on this. Preparation must be made several weeks in advance to ensure the documents arrive on time. It will then be necessary to arrange for your vet to come out within forty-eight hours of travelling to check the horse and sign the papers.

Entry to some countries requires blood tests to be done. Again your vet or shipping agent will advise when necessary. Plan well ahead as it can take up to four weeks to obtain results.

All paper work should be filed in a large envelope or file along with the horse's passport. This should be double checked before departure. It will be needed during the journey so should not be packed where it is difficult to reach.

HEALTH

All horses are at risk of becoming ill during long distance travel. Even with the best care many will suffer from shipping related illness during or after the journey. This can vary from a mild infection to travel sickness, otherwise known as pneumonia. This is very serious and if not diagnosed and treated in the early stages can have detrimental effects on athletic performance and at worse result in death. A number of factors can contribute to illness including:

Stress
This is the main cause of shipping related illness. Having an adverse effect on the immune system puts the horse at a great risk of infection. Bacteria that live in the upper respiratory tract multiply when the horse travels. Tying the horse up with his head elevated allows for the accumulation of these bacteria in the lower respiratory tract, predisposing the risk of infection to the lungs. The digestive system may also suffer as the gut relies on routine and regular feeding. This is not always possible during travel and often when offered food the horse will be reluctant to eat.

Stress can also lead to diarrhoea which could dehydrate the horse. Feeding a probiotic before, during and after travel may eliminate the problem. It is also advisable to feed low energy feeds before and during travel. The horse will have limited exercise for a number of days and feeding too much starch may lead to colic or azoturia.

Enviroment

Poor air circulation and lack of fresh air accompanied by manure and urine build-up will encourage bacterial and fungal growth. This puts the horse at risk of respiratory infection. Conditions are made worse in hot humid weather or when the vehicle is stationary. The horsebox should be as dust free as possible. Any old feed and bedding must be removed and the area thoroughly cleaned. Power hosing will remove old particles of hay containing fungal spores. Dust-free bedding should be used; more will be required than on a short trip.

Dehydration

The horse can survive for longer periods without food than he can without water. Horses that refuse to drink during long journeys are at high risk of becoming dehydrated. This is not good in any instance but more so when the horse is expected to perform at his destination. If this is anticipated it is advisable to seek advice from your vet. He may suggest putting fluids and electrolytes into your horse before departure. This could be done intravenously or by stomach tube. In my experience it has been post competition that horses have suffered more. Often the horse is dehydrated before travel due to the stress of competition. Whenever possible I like my horses to have at least two hours rest after competition before setting off on a long journey. This gives them time to drink, stale and mentally relax. This only applies when they are stabled, there would be no value in standing on the lorry to rest. Electrolytes should be given before, during and after a long journey. They can be administered in the feed or water. For fussy horses it may be necessary to use a syringe.

Sick horses

Where health papers are required it is the vet's responsibility to assess that the horse is fit to travel. When health papers are not required we must make that decision. Horses that are carrying even the mildest strain of a virus are at a severe risk of becoming seriously ill if made to travel. Unfortunately not all infected horses show clinical symptoms, especially early on. It is advisable to monitor the temperature for a week up to departure. If in any doubt it is not worth the risk. Even if the journey goes well performance will undoubtedly be affected.

Weight

Weight loss is a good indicator as to how dehydrated or stressed your horse is after travelling. If you have a weigh bridge it is useful to weigh before and after travel. If this is done consistently even for shorter journeys it will give you an indication of which horses may be a potential problem on a long journey. Measures can then be taken to avoid this.

Additional requirements for long journeys

FEED

All feed needed for the journey should be easily accessible. I find it easier to prepare the feeds beforehand and put them in to small bags. Water containers should be filled and stored with buckets where they can be easily reached during the journey.

RUGS

It is likely that the horse will need a change of rugs during the journey. Rugs should be stored in a convenient place.

THERMOMETERS

Thermometers must be easy to get to. It is advisable to carry a spare one. The temperature should be taken at the first sign that all is not well.

PREPARATIONS FOR LOADING

- All preparations for travel must be made prior to the horses being loaded. This will minimize the time the horses are on board.
- The horse should be suitably dressed. Difficult loaders may need to wear more than a headcollar. This will be discussed.
- The horsebox must be parked in a safe and suitable site.
- Aim to have the ramp as sloping as possible. Parking on a downhill slope will make the ramp less steep. It should also be level and not rock from side to side when the horse stands on it. Loading bays are invaluable for young stock.
- Avoid slippery surfaces.
- When anticipating difficult horses, enclose the entry to the horsebox as much as possible. Parking up to a wall or hedge will eliminate one exit. Reversing into an indoor school or barn entrance often helps.
- Avoid loading in busy areas that offer distractions such as horses walking past or traffic. It is never wise to be close to parked cars
- Always allow sufficient time for loading. Even with good horses it can take longer than you think. If you are uncertain as to how a new horse may be I would advise a practice before the day of the competition. A problem horse could have you running hours late.
- All partitions should be opened as wide as possible. The area should be well lit. Trailers with front unload should have the ramp down to offer more light. The partition can be pulled across to create a wider space to walk in to.

Loading procedure

Loading experienced horses that travel as part of their routine should be an uncomplicated task. It is not a problem for a competent person to do it single handed. However, I do advise that you always familiarize yourself with the horsebox beforehand. When working alone it is important the partitions are quickly closed and secured as soon as the horse is loaded.

- The horse should be led from the shoulder.
- Make a wide approach to the ramp, allowing at least five strides on a straight line.

- Have a good positive walk. If the horse is half asleep he will often trip on the ramp or struggle to get up. He will remember this as a bad experience.
- Walk up the ramp beside the horse. Look straight ahead, not at him.
- If the horse is travelling sideways as he reaches his space pull his head towards you and touch him at his girth area. This will encourage the hindquarters to move over.
- Avoid allowing the horse to put his head over to the horse in the next stall. This can often make it very difficult to turn him.
- Once in the correct place, tie him up and quickly close the partition.
- Only experienced horses should be tied up before the partition is closed. The danger being the horse may panic and pull back. This is a greater risk for horses travelling forwards. It may be necessary in some horseboxes or trailers to leave the head and go to the rear to close the partition or ramp. Until the horse is familiar with the system it is safer to have an assistant.
- Always tie to either string or a quick release rope. Check the rope is long enough to allow the head to be in a normal position and not fixed too high. It should not be so long that he can put his head on the floor or reach other horses.
- Once loading is complete have a last check that all is in order. Lockers and doors should be locked. Windows should be open for ventilation.
- The ramp should be put up at the last possible moment. Always check it has been properly secured. I have known ramps to fall down once the lorry has moved off.

Difficult loaders

Horses can be difficult to load for various reasons including having had a bad experience loading, travelling, unloading. Bad handling, not wanting to leave other horses, fear of small spaces and fear of the unknown are also common reasons for this problem.

It is worth spending time curing the problem as it is an inconvenience. Attempting to train your horse on the day of the competition is not ideal. There is not the time and the horse does not need the added stress. The most important factor is to have more time than your horse. In other words it may take a lot of time and patience to do a good job and build up the horse's confidence. It is not advisable to try single-handed but I feel having too many people causes distractions and can make matters worse.

Some important points to remember when loading are:

- The horsebox or trailer should be parked in the most suitable place as discussed.

- The inside should be well lit.

- The ramp should be as sloping and steady as possible. Metal and wooden ramps are very loud and this noise may deter the horse. Matting can be used to resolve this.

- Open all partitions to make the space inside as big as possible.

- The handler should wear strong, non-slip boots and gloves.

- The horse should have leg protection.

- A headcollar does not offer sufficient control. Other options are a lunge cavesson, bridle with lunge line or a pressure halter. I have found the most effective to be the pressure halter if used the correct way. The halter is designed with pressure points. When the horse is relaxed and working forward with the handler no pressure is applied. If the horse resists or goes against the handler the halter will tighten, applying pressure. The handler must hold the rope steady until the horse decides to move forward, and then be quick to release the pressure. It is important never to pull on the halter when the horse is standing still or moving forward. The same system should apply when using the cavesson or bridle.

- Before attempting to load your horse it is helpful if he has had some education from the ground. Spend some time working him in hand. He must walk with you, halt obediently and move away from you. He should also learn to respect your personal space.

- Start by leading the horse purposefully towards the ramp.

- When he resists, stand still and allow him to settle.

- He must learn that his options are to stand still or go forward, not to go backwards or sideways.

- When he goes forward he is rewarded by the pressure being taken off. I am not against feeding a treat.

- Your assistant can help by keeping him straight. The horse however must stay focused on you and not what is going on around him.

- Once he has reached the ramp allow him to drop his head and smell the ramp.

- If he can't be encouraged to take a step onto the ramp the assistant can lift one front leg followed by the other. The handler can keep the horse's attention by feeding him.
- Once the horse has got this far he may be encouraged to continue up the ramp or he may decide he would rather go home. If it is the latter it must be made to feel uncomfortable for him. Eventually he will make the choice that it is a better experience to go forward.
- Sometimes it helps if the assistant is behind the horse with a schooling or lunge whip. The timing of when this is used is important if the horse is to learn through choice. As with the halter the horse must only feel the whip when he is going backwards. Care must also be taken not to get kicked.
- This process can often be lengthy but usually successful if done correctly.
- Once loaded, the partition should be moved across and the horse tied up.
- Give a small feed to reward and settle the horse.
- Leave him for about twenty minutes with a haynet.
- If he is very unsettled load another horse for company.
- This should be repeated every day until the horse loads willingly first time.

Some horses have the opposite problem and prefer to rush into the lorry. This can become dangerous for the handler. It is often safer to allow the horse to load himself. Approach the ramp with the lead rope over the horse's neck. As he goes to rush allow him to go on his own. Quickly fasten the breeching strap and ramp on a trailer or follow the horse up the ramp and close the partition.

Unloading

- As with loading park in a safe and suitable area. Some horses unload quickly; enough space should be allowed to enable them to continue in a straight line as they may slip if having to turn sharply.
- Experienced horses should not be a problem and it is possible to unload single-handed.
- Let the ramp down.
- Open the partition.

Care should be taken when unloading after a long journey

- Untie the horse. Lead him down the ramp staying at his shoulder.
- If the horse is impatient to leave it may be necessary to have one person untie and hold while the other opens the partition.
- Never rush a horse that is reluctant to unload. As with loading be patient and give him time. Avoid standing in front of him as he may decide to rush or jump.

- Try to stay with the horse if he rushes. Feeding him may help to slow him down.
- After a long journey the horse may be 'jelly legged'. Take time to unload. When leading down the ramp hold the rope quite short with your hand close to the head. This will offer some support.

CARE DURING TRAVELLING

Short journeys – up to two hours

Most horses travel well on short trips. If travelling frequently it becomes part of their routine. An experienced person can safely travel with their horse alone for up to two hours. It is advisable to have roadside cover and carry a mobile phone. If at any time you hear or feel the horse become unsettled, pull over immediately and check the situation. Any horse known to be a bad traveller must be checked frequently. It is not practical for the driver to do this and therefore it is helpful to have an assistant. Never ignore a disturbance from the horse, even if you have almost reached your destination. I have witnessed too often people arriving at competitions with their horses upside down in the horsebox or trailer.

It is not always necessary to give a haynet. I tend not to when galloping or for very short trips. I do prefer to when leaving early and the morning hay has not been fed. It will help to keep the gut in good order. The horse will settle better and not be so grumpy towards the other horses. When travelling to a competition I usually feed 2.7kg (6lb) of haylage. This will not affect performance as you are not likely to go cross-country for at least four hours.

Long journeys

The horse must have more care and attention when travelling long distances. The following must be monitored frequently.

TEMPERATURE IN THE LORRY

This will change throughout a journey depending on number of horses on board, time of day, delays and change of climate. The important factor is to keep as much air circulating as possible. If the temperature feels cold, ventilation must not be closed. More rugs must be applied. In hot humid conditions all possible ventilation must be made available including opening skylights.

TEMPERATURE OF HORSES

Horses that become very stressed when travelling will change temperature frequently. Others may warm up as the journey goes on. It is vital that you check regularly they are not too hot or cold and change rugs accordingly. It will become hotter when the vehicle is stationary and may be necessary to remove rugs during this period.

DRINKING

In my experience very few horses drink sufficient whilst travelling, usually due to stress. To avoid dehydration we must do our best to encourage the horse. Water should be offered every two hours during the journey. Often they will be reluctant to drink whilst on the move. During rest periods remove the haynet and leave a bucket of water with the horse and he may eventually be tempted. Some horses are encouraged if the water is flavoured so try adding apple juice, molasses or glucose. Another option is to float apples in the bucket; once he has wet his lips he may take a drink. Some horses like to 'dunk' their hay into the water. If the bucket can be safely secured, leave half full during travel. This will provide some fluid.

EATING

I prefer to feed haylage as opposed to hay as it is healthier for the respiratory system. Hay must be soaked which can be inconvenient. Not many horses eat quickly during travel so I tend to keep the haynets topped up. The intake of fibre will help to keep the digestive system healthy. For journeys longer than eight hours it will be necessary to feed a concentrate feed to the performance horse. It is advisable prior and during travel to keep the starch intake low. The horse will be doing very little exercise and could cause digestive disorders. It is ideal to feed during rest periods. Try to encourage drinking beforehand. If the horse is reluctant it may help to give a small portion of food and then offer water. It may help to feed the concentrates as a mash or add very sloppy sugar beet pulp. If he refuses to entertain food don't be too worried. It is much more important that he is drinking well.

TRAVEL BY SEA

The horsebox is loaded onto the hold of the ship and all horses remain on the lorry throughout the trip. Livestock are not permitted to sail in bad weather conditions therefore the crossing is usually very smooth.

Whenever possible the ramp should be let down for the duration of the trip to allow as much fresh air as possible. You will not be permitted to stay on the car decks during sailing. The doors will often be locked to prevent you getting back to your vehicle. If the journey is longer than two hours, or you are worried about your horse, it is necessary to make arrangements for an escort to accompany you down.

The temperature is usually quite warm and remains so for the duration of the crossing. I usually leave the horses in a lightweight cooler.

Some horses are unsettled during loading as it can be very noisy and unfamiliar to them. Once sailing, most relax. It is a much smoother ride for them than by road. Offer water and give a small feed to help settle. The horse should then be left with a well-secured, full bucket of water along with a full haynet. If there is space in the lorry, the partitions can be moved to provide more room. Checks should be made every two hours, the horses watered and fed as necessary. If possible skip out, this will help the environment and prevent the risk of thrush in the hind feet. Care must be taken if the horse is wearing bandages. The legs may become swollen due to lack of circulation. The bandages may then become too tight. If possible remove the bandages and massage the legs before re-applying.

REST PERIODS

Ideally the horse should not travel for more than eight hours without a rest period. When the journey is taking over sixteen hours it will be necessary to stable the horses for a longer period of about eight hours. I would advise in this case that you plan your travel through a shipping agent, who will arrange suitable stabling en route. Your agent will also advise on mandatory rest periods and transporting regulations for different countries.

Short rest

- It can often be difficult to find a suitable stopping place at the side of the road. Ideally it should not be too busy and if possible safe to unload.
- The ramp should be dropped and doors opened to allow as much fresh air as possible.
- Whenever possible unload the horses to allow for a leg stretch.
- Grazing for thirty minutes will help clear the airways.
- Safety must come first and this should only be done in a quiet area off the road. Strong or unsettled horses must always wear a bridle.
- Remove bandages or leg wraps. If it is not possible to unload, massage the front legs to improve circulation.
- Take the horse's temperature.
- Offer fresh water.
- Give a small feed if due.
- Muck out the horsebox. Remove droppings and urine. Add clean bedding if necessary.
- Encourage the horse to stale if he has not done so during the journey. Observe the colour of the urine. Thick yellow or brown indicates dehydration.
- Diarrhoea may also lead to dehydration. It is advisable to carry probiotics that can be administered by syringe. These can then be given during the journey even if the horse is not eating.
- If this is suspected do a skin pinch test.
- In the case of the horse dehydrating, the vet must be located immediately on arrival
- Observe the horse in general. He should be alert and interested in his surroundings. Behaviour other than normal should be reported to the vet.

Care after travelling or during longer rest periods

- On arrival at competition or resting stables lower the ramp and check the horses.
- Unload horses. Remove leg and tail protection. Allow the horse to stretch his legs and graze to clear the airways. It is normal to see a white

discharge from both nostrils after long periods of travel. This should not be a thick yellow or green colour and should clear quickly once the head has been down and the horse blows his nose.

- If possible someone can prepare the stables while the horses are grazing.
- Bed down or check bedding is suitable if already for you. Remove any feed or hay that has been left over. Check around the stable for nails or other sharp objects.
- Fill two water buckets, one plain and one with electrolytes. If buckets are provided remove and use your own. They may have been used by infected horses. If there is an automatic drinker in the stable this should be blocked off as it is important to monitor how much the horse is drinking. If the horse has not drunk well during the journey and is still reluctant to drink it is advisable to discuss with the vet. It is important to have the horse hydrated before asking him to perform. He may suggest administering fluids intravenously or by tubing.
- Prepare feed and haylage, again feed from your own manger.
- Prepare stable rugs and bandages.
- Tie the horse up in the stable and take his temperature. If the temperature is normal at this stage it is no guarantee the horse won't get sick, it is not uncommon for them to go downhill two to three days after. Continue to monitor the temperature for the duration of competition and for three to four days after arriving back home.
- If all is well, remove rugs and untie. Allow the horse to roll, stale and drink. If the stable is very small it may be preferable to apply stable bandages before letting him roll.
- Quickly brush off and rug up. Horses are often prone to 'breaking out' shortly after travel so don't rug too heavily at this stage.
- Feed and haylage – give the food from the ground rather than a haynet. This gives more chance to lower the head.
- Observe the behaviour of your horse. It is normal to be unsettled in a strange environment. If he is interested in what is going on around and quite active it is likely he is feeling well. If he is dull and quiet, uninterested in food, water and new surroundings, he is more likely to be ill. Continue to monitor temperature every half hour. If this goes above 102°F call the vet immediately. Early treatment may prevent the illness becoming more serious. The vet will probably administer antibiotics. If

the problem occurs during the journey to a competition it is necessary to inform the vet where the horse is travelling to and what level and discipline he is intending to perform at. In mild cases when the horse is allowed to continue travel, the vet must supply you with information of treatment for the competition vet or your own vet at home.

- If you suspect your horse is sick on arrival at the competition it may be tempting to monitor him yourself and not seek the vet's advice for fear of being eliminated from the competition. Often people think the horse will get over it in a few days and be fit to compete. This is not wise. It is highly unlikely the horse will perform well. Travel sickness does not cure itself and if not treated can permanently effect the horse's athletic performance and at worse be fatal. It is much better to accept the loss of one competition and save your horse for another day.

CHAPTER 9

Competition Preparation

Competition preparation will vary depending on the level and type of competition. Some disciplines are seasonal, therefore planning may need to be done pre-season. Major competitions obviously require more effort but no matter how small the event, your horses should always be 'turned out' to a high standard.

PRE-SEASON PREPARATION

This is the period leading up to the competition when horses are being prepared for shows or events. Now is the time to renew horse registrations and memberships – do this in good time to ensure information and entry forms are returned in time to submit entries.

Make a plan of competitions you intend to enter. It is advisable to have several options, often problems with the horse or balloting will interrupt your programme. Make a note in your diary of when each entry has to be submitted.

All repairs to tack and equipment should be done before your horses come back into work. Competition tack should be brought out of storage, thoroughly cleaned and checked for damage and wear. Repairs can then be made in plenty of time.

Horseboxes and trailers should be serviced and any necessary repairs done. Often internal fittings do not winter well and these should be thoroughly checked for safety before travelling horses.

Horses

- Check teeth.

- Ensure vaccinations are up to date. It is advisable to have flu jabs done during the off season to prevent interference with the work or competition schedule. Certain disciplines do not permit you to compete for seven days after a flu jab is given.

- Blood test – this can prove useful if tests are carried out throughout the season. It is necessary to have a test done when the horse is in good health, to be able to compare. A good time for this is usually pre-season. Routine blood tests (such as a haematology) will indicate if the horse is suffering from a virus or anaemia, this is quite common with the competition horse and can affect performance.

- Plan shoeing dates around competitions. It is not advisable to have your horse shod the day before a competition. Make a note of when you will need stud holes. This may be before the competition season starts if you are planning on show jump and cross-country schooling.

- Fittening programme – this must be individual to each horse taking the following into consideration: ultimate competition goal for the season; date of first competition; level of fitness before rest; length of rest period; health/ injuries; weight; age; type/breed/temperament.

  Decide ultimately how fit your horse needs to be and set a target date to achieve this. Work back from this to decide when your programme needs to start. It is much easier to get a horse fit that you know well than a horse that is new to you. Setbacks such as lameness or a virus are likely to happen at some point along the way. Allow for this by giving yourself extra time. It is much easier to give an easy week to a fit horse than trying to rush things which is likely to cause injury.

- Diary – make a daily report on each horse. Include work programme, health, soundness, feed and weights. This is useful to look back on, especially from season to season.

Preparation – two weeks leading up to competition

The amount of preparation will depend on the following

- Type of competition
- Number of horses competing
- Distance travelling
- Length of time away

TACK AND EQUIPMENT

- All tack should be repaired and ready to use. The fit of tack not used on a daily basis should be checked prior to the competition.
- Numnahs and girths to be checked and washed.
- Boots and bandages to be checked and washed.
- Rugs washed or cleaned. Whenever possible have clean stable rugs to take on overnight stays.
- Stable equipment cleaned and labelled.
- Feed, hay/haylage, supplements ordered.
- First aid box checked and complete.
- Ensure feet and shoes in good condition. Stud holes where necessary. A spare set of shoes should be obtained for each horse.
- Manes and tails pulled. Feathers trimmed. Clipped if necessary.
- Practise plaiting manes and tails if you find it a struggle. It is not wise to find out you can't do it on the morning of a competition.
- Travel arrangements – plan well ahead for long or overseas trips. The vet will need to be arranged to sign health papers.
- Make a check list of everything you will need. Buy what you don't have before the competition rather than relying on being able to get it at the competition.
- The following check list is suitable for a three-day event. It will cover most of the equipment needed for other disciplines.

TACK

- BRIDLES – Dressage, show jump and cross-country. If the same bridle is used for all three disciplines, a spare one should be packed.
- BITS – Dressage, show jump and cross-country
- HUNTING BREASTPLATE
- AINTREE BREASTPLATE

- MARTINGALE or ATTACHMENT
- SPARE CROSS-COUNTRY REINS
- SPARE REIN STOPS
- SADDLES – Dressage, show jump and cross-country
- NUMNAHS/SADDLE CLOTHS - Dressage, show jump and cross-country. Work numnahs x 2
- RISER PADS
- GIRTHS – Dressage, show jump and cross-country. Work girths x 2
- STUD GUARD
- OVER GIRTH x 2
- SPARE CROSS-COUNTRY LEATHERS AND IRONS
- BOOT LACE – To tie bridle on
- TROT UP CHAIN
- LUNGE EQUIPMENT – Cavesson. Lunge line. Roller. Side reins. Whip
- GADGETS
- FLY NET
- EAR SOCKS
- CHAMOIS LEATHER – Helps prevent the saddle slipping back
- BRIDLE NUMBERS
- HOLE PUNCH

BOOTS/BANDAGES

- DRESSAGE – Smart set to warm up for dressage and trot up
- CROSS-COUNTRY x 2 sets
- SHOW JUMPING
- OVER REACH x 2 sets
- WORK BOOTS x 2 sets
- TUBI-GRIP
- STABLE BANDAGES AND UNDER WRAPS x 2 sets
- TAIL BANDAGES x 3

EXTRA EQUIPMENT

- STUD BOX – 3 sets of each type of stud (more will be required if a number horses are competing at the same time). Tap x 2. Bradal or nail. Spanner. Cotton wool/plugs. WD40. Hoof pick x 2
- SPARE SHOES/PADS

- TALCUM POWDER
- TAPE x 4 rolls
- BUCKETS x 4 (for washing down)
- LARGE SPONGES x 4
- TOWELS x 8
- SPARE NYLON HEADCOLLAR AND ROPE
- GREASE/RUBBER OR PLASTIC GLOVES FOR APPLYING
- BOOT POLISH/BRUSHES/CLOTH

STABLE EQUIPMENT

- FORK
- BROOM
- SHOVEL
- SKIP
- WHEELBARROW/MUCK SACK (The wheelbarrow is very useful for carrying equipment as stables may not be close to the horsebox park)
- HAY SOAKING BIN
- BEDDING – If not provided
- WATER BUCKETS x 2
- HOOKS TO HANG BUCKETS
- FEED BUCKETS x 2
- HAYNETS x 2
- MUZZLE
- GROOMING KIT
- PLAITING KIT
- HOOF OIL AND BRUSH
- BABY OIL
- SHAMPOO
- FLY SPRAY
- SAFETY PINS
- SEWING KIT
- TACK CLEANING EQUIPMENT – Saddle soap. Oil. Metal polish. Sponges. Cloths
- SADDLE RACK
- BRIDLE HOOKS
- RUG RACK

- STRING
- TORCH
- STAPLE GUN
- BIN LINERS – Wash bags
- WATER CONTAINERS

TRAVEL EQUIPMENT

- HEAD COLLAR AND ROPE
- POLL GUARD
- RUGS
- ROLLER
- TAIL BANDAGE
- TAIL GUARD
- TRAVEL BANDAGES AND WRAPS/TRAVEL BOOTS

FEED

- CONCENTRATES
- HAY/HAYLAGE
- SUPPLEMENTS/ELECTROLYTES
- FEED CHART
- FEED SCOOP

Always take extra feed and hay. Some competitions may provide feed. When possible use your own feed as digestive disorders may occur from a sudden change of feed.

RUGS

- STABLE
- COOLERS x 3
- DAY RUG
- SUMMER SHEET
- WATER PROOF
- EXERCISE SHEET
- ROLLERS
- HOOD/NECK COVER
- TAIL BAG

FIRST AID KIT

- THERMOMETERS x 2
- DRESSINGS – Robinson Skintact and Activate
- SURGICAL BANDAGES – Equiwrap, Flexoplast
- COTTON WOOL
- GAMGEE
- ELASTOPLAST
- ANIMALINTEX
- KAOLIN POULTICE
- STERILE BOWL AND TRAY
- SCISSORS x 2
- TWEEZERS
- ANTISEPTIC WASH, POWDER, CREAM
- TETCIN SPRAY
- EPSOM SALTS
- WITCH HAZEL
- ARNICA – OINTMENT AND PILLS
- VASELINE
- ELECTROLYTES
- SYRINGE
- EQUIBOOT
- HOOF TESTERS
- TUBBING BUCKET
- TAPE
- HOSE
- ICE BOOTS
- JEY CLOTHS
- TUBI GRIPS
- ICE TIGHT
- MAGNETIC BOOTS/RUG

DOCUMENTS

- PASSPORT/VACCINATION CERTIFICATE
- TRAVEL DOCUMENTS
- HEALTH PAPERS
- SCHEDULE

- MAP/DIRECTIONS
- DRESSAGE TESTS
- RULE BOOK
- DIARY

Preparation – the day before

As much preparation as is possible should be done during the week leading up to the competition to ensure the day before runs smoothly. Make a list of jobs that are to be done during the day and aim to finish early, allowing horses and yourself an early night. This may mean an early start!

HORSES

Try to work the horses in the morning. This will give you the rest of the day to get things ready.

The horse can be turned out for a period while tack and equipment is prepared and he will need a thorough groom or a bath. If weather permits bathing the horse will have a better result. Clipped horses can be hot clothed.

Wash the mane. It can be difficult to plait a freshly washed mane, especially if the hair is very fine. To avoid this wash the mane a few days prior to plaiting.

Wash the tail. Again if it is to be plaited the top of the tail may need washing earlier. Brush the tail out and apply conditioner, avoid the top of the tail if it is to be plaited. Plait the tail down and leave over night to avoid dirt and bedding. A tail bandage should be applied to a pulled tail for a few hours each day to improve appearance.

White socks need to be washed and dried off and stable bandages can be applied to keep the legs clean. Scrub feet inside and out. Check shoes are secure and clenches are not risen.

Trim the bridle path; trim, shave or clip the whiskers

Clean the stud holes and re-plug. If the horse is prone to being difficult with his feet, the tap should not be used when standing on concrete. If the horse stamps his foot down the tap will snap, leaving half of it in the hole. This can be extremely difficult to remove without taking off the shoe. Taps with rubber backs are available to avoid this.

It may be necessary to plait the day before if you have a very early start

or several horses to get ready. This should not be done until later in the day. Horses that suffer from sweet itch should never be plaited the night before. Tails must not be plaited the night before.

Rug up according to weather conditions. Hoods or neck covers will help keep the horse clean and protect the mane if it is plaited. Tail bags are useful for grey horses. Tail bandages should not be left on overnight.

It is advisable to trot the horse up to make sure he is sound and finally weigh the horse if you have a weigh bridge.

EQUIPMENT

All tack should be stripped, checked and thoroughly cleaned with special attention being made to reins, cheek pieces, stirrup leathers, girths and girth straps. Scrub rubber reins and stirrup treads. Make sure that all equipment is put back together correctly and fitted to the horse. Stirrup leathers should be the correct length. This will help if the horse is very fresh when first ridden.

Polish all brass, including brass on leather headcollars.

Pack the horsebox using the check list to tick things off as they go in. It may be a security risk to leave tack in overnight in which case you must allow sufficient time for this task in the morning. Consider equipment that you may need during the journey and ensure it is easily accessible. Highlight on your check list any equipment that is to be packed the next day to ensure it is not forgotten.

Check that the partitions and head boards are in their correct place. Put bedding down for travelling, fill haynets, water tank/containers.

Prepare travel equipment for the horses but leave out necessary grooming, plaiting and washing equipment that will be needed the next day.

Check oil, water and diesel. If leaving very early it may be necessary to fill up with diesel the night before. Check the horsebox will start. Check lights on trailers. Pack all rider equipment.

Phone for starting times. Plan your journey. Work out how long it will take to get there. In winter check the weather forecast.

Make a list of jobs that need to be the next day before departure. Plan what time you need to start. Give yourself fifteen minutes extra as it is better to have more time than not enough.

CHAPTER 10

Care of the Horse at a Competition

All horses become stressed during competition, some more than others. Change in routine, travelling, nerves or excitement all contribute to the change in temperament. You may find some horses improve with age and experience; others are affected more as the demands of performance and fitness become greater.

In taking care of the horse during competition, it is our role to minimize the causes of physical and mental stress. We must learn to recognize the symptoms and not all horses react in the same way – some become very excited and difficult to handle whilst others become withdrawn, refusing to eat or drink. It is important to know your horse's personality at home to be able to compare behaviour at a competition. For example, one horse I have has a very independent character when he is at home. He likes his 'own space' and will put his ears back when you enter his stable. At a competition he becomes a different horse, calling for me over the stable door and pricking his ears when I go to him. This is not because he is happy to be at a competition! This is a sign of stress; he is showing his insecurity in a strange environment. This is just one example of the many ways a horse will react.

In order to keep our horses relaxed, we must be relaxed ourselves as we work around them. Organization and time keeping are the key factors to ensure the day runs smoothly. We must prepare beforehand and ensure we are

A team of horses ready to travel

on time. If we are disorganized and rushing around the horse mistakes will be made and the horses are likely to become unsettled. Your horse may not be as easy to work with as he is at home. Never lose your temper as this will make matters worse and certainly does not appear professional in the public eye. Make your motto 'Calmness comes through discipline', be firm, sympathetic and patient.

If you tend not to be good at time keeping, set your watch ten minutes fast and this should ensure you are on time. If you have a tendency to forget things, make check lists and reminders for the day. The job will become easier as you gain practice and experience.

The general care of the horse is the same for all types of competition but routine and preparation will vary slightly. Care of the horse at a one-day event is slightly different to that required at a pure dressage or show jumping show. The horse has to be prepared for three different disciplines.

What follows is an example of a competition taking place on one day, including travelling there and home. This is a routine I use, it may not suit all types of competition but can be used as a guide and check list. It is important to develop your own system as you become more experienced at competition grooming.

BEFORE DEPARTURE

- Make a list of jobs that need doing before you leave.
- Consider potential problems. For example, a problem loader or a grey horse covered in stable stains. The day does not get off to a good start if you are late leaving. There will be a more relaxed atmosphere if you are driving out twenty minutes early rather than half an hour late.
- On arrival on the yard check all horses and feed. Leave to eat. Most horses are very sensitive to change, if you start to fuss over them while they are eating it may put them off their food.
- Finish packing the horsebox and make a final check everything is in.
- Lower ramp and adjust partitions ready for loading.
- Muck out yard if you don't have people at home to do it.
- Groom and check the horse over. Be observant to legs and feet. There is nothing more sickening than driving three hours to a competition to discover you have a lame horse.
- If in any doubt about soundness, always trot up. When leaving for a three-day event this should be a matter of routine.
- Remove all stable stains.
- Plait.
- Prepare to travel.
- Load.
- Make a final check before leaving.

Care during travel is discussed in chapter 8.

ARRIVAL AT COMPETITION

The amount of time you have before the first phase will vary from one event to another. You must consider the following: does the rider have to walk the course before the dressage? Allow sufficient time to collect numbers. How long does the horse need to work in? If you have more than one horse and times are very close it may be necessary to work all the horses before the dressage starts.

On arrival drop the ramp, check the horses (including rugs). Offer them water. Note how much hay/haylage they have eaten. Unless you have a very long wait it is advisable to remove haynets.

If time permits it is a good idea to unload the horses and allow them to graze for a short period. This will assist in clearing the airways after travelling with the head tied up. It is normal to see discharge from the nostrils when the horse puts his head down and they may give the odd cough. Symptoms should not persist after the horse has grazed for a short period. If the horse is not allowed to lower his head and is ridden immediately, he will often be irritated in his wind, causing him to cough and blow his nose. It is worth allowing a little extra time for horses that are prone to this as it may affect performance.

Prepared for travel

Skip out the horsebox as the horses are unloaded and continue to keep the area clean throughout the day. Muck must be taken home with you and not dumped in the lorry park.

Write out each horse's number and section and all the times for the day. This is easier to follow if done in order. It should be pinned up where it is easy to see.

EXAMPLE
BLUE – 52 – B
BLACKIE – 123 – C
PATCH – 337 – G

9.07 – BLUE – D
10.15 – BLACKIE – D
11.30 – BLUE – SJ
12.37 – PATCH – D
13.23 – BLACKIE – SJ
14.47 – BLUE – XC
15.32 – BLACKIE – XC
16.08 – PATCH – SJ
16.50 – PATCH – XC

Discuss each horse's programme with the rider. Consider how long is needed for warming up for each phase and if you need to lunge before the dressage.

Work out what time each horse needs to be ready for each phase and aim to be ready five minutes early. If you have a number of horses and helpers discuss each person's responsibilities. The most senior person must always do a final check on tack and equipment.

At some point the rider will need to walk the cross-country course. It is not always possible to walk with them if you have a number of horses to look after. If the opportunity does arise, do so. It is interesting to see what the horses are expected to jump. It will also give you an idea where to go if the rider or horse are unfortunate enough to have a fall and you are needed to go out onto the course to assist. Before going to walk make sure the horses are comfortable and wearing the suitable rugs. Do not leave equipment lying around outside the horsebox.

Numbers will need to be collected. Check how much the start fee is and if you are required to produce your vaccination certificate or medical card.

*When possible walk
the course and watch
the horse go cross-
country*

Unload equipment from the horsebox to give you space to work in. Fill the water buckets and in hot weather stand them in the shade.

If you have time before the dressage it may benefit the horse to walk him in-hand around the lorry park. It is not wise to take a horse close to the competition area as he may become excited. Difficult horses should be led in a bridle and lunge line.

DRESSAGE

Preparation
Prepare equipment – Bridle

Breastplate (optional)

Saddle

Saddle cloth

Riser pad

Boots

Studs

If the weather permits it is easier to get the horse ready outside. There must be a suitable place to tie up and the horse should not be prone to 'pulling back'. If you have an assistant they can hold the horse. Tie short to prevent grazing. Eating at this stage will cause the bit to become very messy.

When working around the horse in the horsebox safety is a priority. Do not put yourself in a dangerous situation, especially around the hind legs. It may not be possible to put on hind boots and studs until you unload. Remove the travel boots and rugs. In cold weather the rugs can be quartered back. Brush off. Check plaits are intact. Remove tail bandage. Brush out the tail, apply baby oil to the bottom. Reapply the tail bandage. Sponge eyes, nose and dock. Apply baby oil to around the eyes and nostrils. Put a suitable rug over the horse.

This is the order I follow when tacking up for each discipline:

- Studs – discuss with rider suitable studs.
- Boots.
- Breastplate.
- Saddle.
- I leave the bridle until the last as the horse may rub and damage the leather.
- Wipe the coat over with a dry stable rubber.
- Apply fly spray if necessary. It is safer to spray onto a cloth and wipe on than to spray directly onto the horse.
- Apply quarter markings.
- Put the bridle on.
- Unload.
- Check the feet are clean and apply hoof oil.
- Keep the horse warm with a rug or walk until the rider is ready to get on.
- Check the girth when the rider has mounted.

At the arena

This is the equipment I would take with me to the dressage area:

Brush

Sponge

Fly repellent

Cloth

Small bottle of water

Copy of dressage test

Each dressage arena will have a steward. Ask your steward which arena you are in and if they are running on time. Inform your rider. When the horse before you starts, remove boots and tail bandage. Check the girth. Give any final touches if necessary. Some horses can be very tense at this stage and do not want to stand still in which case it is better to keep working them and not have to stop. If this is the case boots cannot be worn to warm up. Remind the rider do drop the whip before entering the arena.

After the test

Take the horse back to the lorry, untack him and sponge off if necessary. Offer him water but no more than half a bucket. Offer more after ten minutes if he is still thirsty If time permits, allow ten minutes grazing to cool the horse. This will also help him relax.

Put away dressage equipment. Dirty boots and the saddle cloth should be put into a wash bag. Tack can be cleaned throughout the day if there is time, if not it will be done at home.

If there is a long break before the show jumping, the horse can be left to relax. Some will settle more on the lorry, whilst others are happier tied up outside. In summer flies are a pest and it is often cooler inside.

Water should be freely available or offered every half hour. Food should not be given at this stage.

SHOW JUMPING

Preparation

- Select tack and equipment – Bridle

    Breastplate

    Martingale (optional)

    Saddle

    Saddle cloth / Pads

    Boots

- Brush and tidy the horse.
- Pick out feet. Check or change studs.
- Tack up.
- Re-apply fly repellent.

The collecting ring

Equipment to take to show jumping – Spare tack (if necessary)

Bottle of water

Stud kit (you may need to change studs if the ground has become bad in the arena).

When you get to the show jumping collecting ring find out how many horses there are to jump before yours. Assist with practice jumps.

Make a final check of the girth before the horse goes into the ring.

After the round

You may need to get ready for the cross-country phase immediately after the show jumping so be well prepared. Remove the tack and boots if you have

Sponge out the mouth if the horse is reluctant to drink

a complete change for cross-country. If the same tack is used, loosen the girth and noseband. Sponge off if necessary. Offer water and again remember that the horse can drink up to half a bucket. If he is reluctant to drink, sponge the mouth. Keep warm with a cooler if necessary, unplait (but this is optional).

CROSS-COUNTRY

Preparation

- Prepare cross country equipment – Bridle

    Breastplate

    Martingale

    Numnah/pads

    Saddle

    Girth/overgirth

    Over reach boots

    Cross-country boots

    Tape/scissors

    Grease (optional)

Check or change studs; tack up or make suitable adjustments to tack.

Whether or not you use grease is down to personal preference. The only advantage I have found is that it may help to protect the stifles if the horse is prone to catching them on drop fences. In cool weather the grease can be applied before the rider mounts. In hot weather it should be done at the last possible moment as it will quickly melt. Apply using rubber or plastic gloves. The reins and stirrup treads must be held well clear. Run a dry towel over the reins and stirrups.

The rider should now mount and walk the horse around. The girth is then tightened. Standing on the near side pass the buckle of the overgirth over the saddle. Thread through the numnah girth loops and through the martingale or breastplate. Check it is lying over the girth and secure tightly.

Have a final check over the equipment before they set off.

Now is the time to get everything ready for after the cross-country. My list includes:

A horse being prepared to go cross-country

The studs may need to be changed for the cross-country

Grease being applied

The groom fastening the overgirth

Four full water buckets

Sponges and sweat scraper

Cooler

Headcollar and rope

Spanner to remove studs

Scissors

Towels

Ice boots into water

Stable bandages and wraps

The cross-country round

Some horses may be difficult to get into the start box. You may be required to assist. Take a lead rope; thread it through the bit ring rather than clipping on. This will be much easier to release. Whenever possible watch the cross-country. If you are busy with another horse it is usually possible to hear the commentary from the lorry park. It is very important you listen to your horse's progress in case there is a problem.

After the cross-country

When the horse finishes, the rider dismounts and you take the horse. Quickly assess his condition. How hard is he blowing? Are there any obvious signs of injury? Loosen the girths and noseband and walk back to the lorry. Observe the recovery rate and how he is walking. Are there any sins of lameness or discomfort?

In very hot weather an assistant can remove the tack and wash while you continue walking. Cooling will speed up the recovery rate. When the horse has stopped blowing hard, remove the tack and wash the neck and body, scrape and apply a rug if necessary. Beware of rugging up too soon; the horse's temperature will continue to rise for up to ten minutes post exercise. Walk again if necessary.

Remove the boots and studs. Wash the legs. Thoroughly check for cuts

and swelling. Observe how the horse is standing. A horse can often pull up sound and not feel an injury until his adrenalin has dropped. Dry the legs off with a towel.

Ice boots can be used to cool the legs and reduce inflammation. I tend only to use them on a horse with a chronic problem or when the ground is very hard. They must be removed after twenty minutes or sooner if they become warm.

Offer the horse water, allowing no more than a third of a bucket; offer every ten minutes until the thirst is quenched.

Wash the head, dry with a towel. Check inside the mouth for cuts at the corners and bruised bars. Plug the stud holes. Hand walk for five to ten minutes. Allow the horse to graze and remove the plaits.

If you are taking care of several horses you may not have time to clean tack and equipment. Dirty boots, girths and numnahs should be put into a bag. Tack can be cleaned when you have time but must be done thoroughly and not rushed over.

Check the horse after forty-five minutes. Change rugs if necessary. Feel

the legs and feet for heat, swelling and pain on pressure. If all looks well, stable bandages can be applied. I tend to bandage horses that have run at Advanced level, ones that are prone to filled legs or all horses when the ground is very hard. Otherwise I do not do anything with the legs. I prefer to see if there is a problem rather than hide it.

Ice boots being applied after the cross-country

Clay and Ice Tight are products which can be used to cool the legs and prevent swelling. This can be an advantage at a three-day event when the legs should look good for the trot up. The danger of using such a product is that it can mask an injury because they are often applied immediately after cross-country before an injury has had a chance to surface. When the clay is removed the following morning the leg will look and feel good. The injury goes unnoticed; work continues causing the problem to become more serious.

The horse can then be prepared to travel and given a haynet. Continue to offer water frequently. If you have a long wait before departure, a small feed can be given. The horse should be allowed to graze as much as possible, rather than standing in the lorry with his head tied up.

During the journey home check him regularly. It may be necessary to change or add rugs. Water should be offered, although few horses will drink during the journey.

STABLING OVER NIGHT

Sometimes it is necessary to stable away from home if you are competing over a number of days or travelling a long distance to a competition. The competition venue may offer stabling, or the secretary will organize stables locally on private yards. When stabling on site you will need to find the stable manager's office, they will then provide you with information. If you are staying at a private yard, a telephone number of your host will be provided along with confirmation of your entry. It is courteous to call beforehand to introduce yourself, give an indication of when you intend to arrive and ask for directions on how to find them.

It is usual to state on the stabling booking form the bedding you require and it is worth checking this over the telephone because once you get there it may be too late to do anything about it. Often straw is the only bedding available and if this does not suit your horse it may be necessary to provide your own. This must be taken into consideration when doing entries as bedding can take up the space of a horse on the lorry.

Arrival at the stables
- Check the horses and drop the ramp.
- Find the owners or person in charge.
- Ask where the following are:

  The stables

  Water supply

  Muck heap

  Tools, for mucking out (provide your own when possible)
- Find out the routine for the yard. If it is possible to feed at the same time it may save upset to the horses. Inform them of your plans; when you intend to leave. When you will return if you are staying more than one night. How would they like the beds left?

- Check the stables for sharp or dangerous objects.

- Check the mangers do not contain leftover feed.

- Remove any leftover hay.

- Check the water is clean. If the stable has an automatic watering system I would still provide a water bucket, the horse may be wary of a strange 'drinker' to start with. Provide two buckets if this is the only source of water.

- Unload the horses. Remove travel equipment.

- If the horse is warm, walk until cool.

- Put the horse in the stable. If he is plaited, avoid allowing him to roll until he has a rug and hood on. This will save you a lot of work trying to recover the plaits, especially if it is a shavings bed.

- It may be wise to apply stable bandages to protect the legs if the stable is small or the horse is prone to rolling a lot.

- Allow the horse to drink and settle.

- Feed. Use your own feed manger rather than the one in the stable. This may have contained illegal substances.

- Clean the horsebox. Prepare travel equipment and haynets for the next morning.

- Refill water tank or containers.

- Clean tack.

- Plait if necessary.

- Check how the horse is drinking and eating. Often they will go off the feed when stabling away. Do not overface with large feeds, give little and often. Feed carrots and apples which may encourage interest in the feed. At this stage drinking is much more important and likely to have a derogatory effect on the performance. In very hot conditions it may be necessary to discuss with the vet at the competition if you are worried in any way.

- The droppings may become very loose as a result of stress upsetting the gut. Feeding a probiotic or live yogurt will help keep the digestive system in good order.

- Be cautious of putting on too many rugs. The body temperature may be higher than usual due to the stress of being in a strange environment. If the horse becomes too hot it will encourage him to roll which puts him at risk of getting cast or injuring himself.

- The water buckets should be checked and refilled as late as possible. In my experience the horse is often reluctant to drink until he has settled and eaten. Following a long journey he will often drink a lot.

- Work out what time you will need to leave the following morning. Make a list of jobs that need doing before departure.

Next day

- Check – The horse in general

    How much has been eaten/drunk

    Droppings

- Fill water buckets

- Remove leftover food

- Feed. Leave the horse to eat if this suits him

- Prepare the lorry for loading

- Muck out

- Groom/plait

- Prepare for travel

- Pack equipment

- Load horses

- Thoroughly tidy stables and yard area

- Thank your hosts for having you

CARE AFTER THE COMPETITION

- Unload

- Remove travel equipment and rugs. Bandages may stay on over night. Check they are still secure or have not become too tight. If they have been on for more than eight hours it is advisable to remove them for twenty minutes and reapply.

- Trot the horse up. If all looks well he can be put in his stable. If he is very hot he should be walked until cool. Otherwise he may roll and get cast.

- Any signs of lameness should be investigated immediately. Applying cold to the area will reduce inflammation. This is probably all you can do at this stage, especially if it is late at night.

- Observe the horse in the stable. Hopefully he will drink and pass urine. If the urine is very dark in colour, it is likely he is dehydrated. Electrolytes should be given in the feed or water. (Discussed in chapter 5.) It is not likely that a horse will suffer badly from dehydration following a one-day event. However drinking should be monitored as slight dehydration may affect performance.
- Once the horse is cool he can have his rugs and bandages put back on.
- Feed
- Unloading and cleaning of the horsebox is better done the following day if it is very late. For security reasons it may be necessary to remove the tack.
- Have a final check on your horses before leaving for the night.

DAY AFTER THE COMPETITION

- Check all horses – How much they have eaten
                    Drinking (this is not possible with automatic drinkers. If you are concerned about the drinking, buckets should be used)
                    State of bed/droppings

- Feed
- Remove bandages. Check for obvious signs of injury. It is difficult to assess the legs when they are warm from the bandages. I allow half an hour for them to cool down, any signs of heat and swelling will then be allowed to surface. If the horse is very warm under his rugs, the legs may stay warm and slightly 'puffy'. Removing the rugs and allowing the horse to cool down will help.
- Thoroughly check the feet and legs for heat, swelling and pain on pressure.
- Remove the rugs and check the condition of the horse.
- Trot up
- Weigh if possible but if not, assess the condition. Excessive loss in condition could indicate dehydration or stress.
- Feel over the back and girth area for rubs, swelling and sensitivity.
- Check the mouth for cuts and bruising.
- Check the shoes.
- Treat any injuries as necessary. Heat and swelling should be treated immediately, especially when in a tendon or joint area. There may not be lameness. If in doubt it is wise to seek the vet's opinion. A slight injury can very soon become serious if ignored and the horse is turned out or work is continued.
- It is normal to give a day off after competition. The horse will benefit from turn out or a hand graze. If he is prone to stiffness a gentle horse walk or hand walk may help.
- Finish unpacking and cleaning the horsebox. Check for any damage, especially to internal fittings.
- All tack should be stripped, checked and thoroughly cleaned. Repairs should be dealt with immediately in order to be ready for the next competition.
- Boots, bandages, numnahs, girths and rugs washed dried and put away.
- Diary updated, recording – Results of competition
  Health
  Fitness
  Weight/condition.
  Treatments
- Consider the horse's competition and fitness programme. It may be

necessary to make changes to future plans and entries that have been done if the horse did not perform as expected.

- Continue to monitor closely your horse for the next few days. Sometimes an injury may take longer to surface. The horse should not be stressed for a few days but will benefit from a quiet hack which will allow you to assess how he has recovered from the competition. Younger or less experienced horses often take longer to recover. It is not unusual for them to be tired for a few days afterwards. If however your horse takes longer than usual to return to normal, he may have picked up a virus. The temperature should be monitored. The vet can take a blood sample. It is most important that you recognize the signs and your horse is fully recovered from one competition before further stress is put on him to prepare for the next.

CHAPTER 11

Care of the Horse at a Three-Day Event

A three-day event is the ultimate test of the event horse; it requires precise preparation aiming for the horse to arrive at the event in good health, sound and at peak fitness. Different from a one-day event, each discipline takes place over separate days and the horses must stay on site for the duration of the event. Each horse must pass a vets' inspection to allow them to start the competition; during the next two days dressage takes place, following that is the speed and endurance, which involves two roads and tracks, steeplechase and the cross-country. The next day there is another vets' inspection to make sure the horses are fit to complete the final show jumping phase. The groom's role at the three-day event is more demanding than most other disciplines. The 'D' box can be compared to a pit stop in Formula One motor racing and a good support team is essential if all is to go well.

Caring for a horse at a three-day event may seem like an easy task, especially for those who look after a number of horses at home but having done it you soon realize that it is both physically and mentally challenging and you tend to arrive back home thoroughly exhausted.

This chapter covers the responsibilities of the groom, problems that may occur during the event and how best to deal with them.

PREPARATION FOR DEPARTURE

Preparing the horse, horsebox and equipment for a three-day event is similar to that for a one-day event. (see chapter 10). There are however other aspects to think about prior to leaving for a three-day event.

When to leave will depend on the distance to get to the event and the temperament of the horse. Some horses may benefit from having more time to settle into their competition environment prior to the event starting; most three-day events usually open the stables three or four days before the event starts and when travelling to a competition in your own country it is normal to leave the day before the trot up, this gives ample time for the horses to recover from the journey. When travelling overseas the horses would need more time to recover therefore an earlier departure is necessary.

Before getting the horses ready to travel, check that legs and feet feel normal and trot up the horse to make sure he is sound. When travelling abroad your vet must check the horse before departure and sign necessary health papers. If it is going to be a long journey the vet may also need to tube or IV fluids into the horse to prevent dehydration (see chapter 8). Have a final check that everything is packed - passport, health documents, event passes etc. If there is space for a bike then it is advisable to take one or you will be doing a lot of walking.

ARRIVAL

On arrival it is usual for the vet to check the horse before it can enter the stables. Drop the ramp of the lorry and check the horses. When the vet arrives you will need to have the horse's passport ready which the vet then keeps until the end of the event. The horse is then unloaded, rugs and boots removed and the vet examines the horse to make sure the horse and passport match. Then let the horse have a walk and a pick of grass before putting him in the stable.

Stabling

Most three-day events use temporary stabling which measures about 3m by 3m (10ft by 10ft); not much space for a big horse! Whatever the stabling it must be checked thoroughly for nails, sharp objects etc before putting the horse in.

BEDDING

When filling in your entry form you would have stated what bedding you required, whenever possible use the same bedding as your horse has at home. The event usually supplies two bales and any extra has to be bought and can be expensive so if you have space on the lorry to bring your own it can be cheaper.

In the case of temporary stables the floor is often grass, if the grass is quite long let the horse eat it before bedding down, otherwise he will dig up the bed to get to the grass.

WATER

The horse must have water available to him at all times. If he rolls a lot or knocks the buckets over it is better to hang them rather than have them on the floor. The horse may drink more than usual so two buckets are advisable and should be checked and monitored frequently. If the horse is not drinking then speak to the vet for advice (chapter 5 advises on drinking and feeding problems).

Feeding

ROUGHAGE

Feed the same rations of hay/haylage as you would at home if not more, especially if the horse usually gets turned out in the field as it will substitute the grass. Fibre will keep the horse occupied, keep the digestive system in order and help prevent dehydration so the more you give the better. If the horse eats very quickly or tends to mix the hay into the bed use a haynet, otherwise I prefer to feed from the floor to aid the respiratory system.

CONCENTRATES

Wherever possible feed the same number of feeds as you would at home. One of the most common problems is horses going off their feed during competitions (discussed in chapter 5) and you may find the horse gains his appetite again as the week goes on and he is more settled. Don't be too worried if the horse doesn't eat much the first few days as long as he is drinking well.

Once the horse is fed, watered and happy in the stable, leave him to rest. You can then organize your equipment. The horsebox will need cleaning out - quite often this becomes a tackroom for the week so clear enough space to allow you to work in there.

It can be a long walk from the horsebox to the stable; keeping some of the equipment in boxes at your stable can save a lot of time. Typically this equipment would include:

Mucking out tools

Grooming kit

Washing down buckets, sponges and scraper

Work boots/bandages

Headcollar

Rugs – a rug rack can be made from string and hung in the stable if the horse does not chew rugs

Stud box

Stable Bandages

Tail bandage.

At some point during the day the horse will be exercised and this will depend on the length of the journey - he may just hack to stretch his legs or he may need to work harder. This would be discussed with the rider, quite often at three-day events a horse is worked more than once throughout the day. Whatever the horse does it is important he comes out groomed, mane and tail laid and looking smart. It is advisable to put on boots or bandages as the horse may be fresh; over-reach boots may also be necessary especially when lungeing.

Numbers

The horse will be given a number. This must be worn at all times when he leaves the stable whether he is ridden, lungeing or hand grazing. Failure to do so will result in elimination.

After working the horse will need washing off or grooming as necessary, pay particular attention to the legs, feet and shoes. If the horse returns from work quite hot hand grazing after washing will help cool and relax him and prevent him rolling in a small stable. Again, when hand grazing it is important to put boots or bandages on the horse as he may be spooky in a strange environment.

When out of the stable the horse should be smartly turned out, wearing a number

Rugs

When rugging up consider the temperature compared to home both inside and outside the stable, the horse may be warmer due to stress. Try to avoid over rugging as this will encourage rolling which is not ideal in small stables. Rugs may need to be changed frequently throughout the day and must be checked on a regular basis.

Stable bandages

If your horse wears stable bandages at home then continue to do so at the event. Also consider using bandages for horses that have a tendency to roll as it will offer some protection. They also help prevent filling and help keep white legs clean.

Tack

Tack should be cleaned and put away ready for the next day – always paying particular attention to stitching. Boots and bandages should be brushed off and anything that has got wet during the course of the day, hung out to dry.

Late check

Always check your horse last thing before going to bed. Skip out the stable, check the water, give more hay if necessary, check rugs and change if necessary and check that the horse has eaten his last feed.

THE TROT UP DAY

The day before the competition officially starts all the horses entered must pass a vets' inspection or 'Trot Up'. Each horse is presented in front of the Ground Jury which usually comprises three members and the vets. The horses must be plaited and turned out immaculately which takes some preparation therefore a plan must be worked out with the rider to give the groom time to get ready.

Planning

To make a plan it is best to work back from the time the trot up starts and this usually runs in numerical order and each horse will take about one minute. You can therefore roughly estimate what time your horse goes.

Aim to be ready half and hour before your time and then consider:

- How many times the horse will be ridden before the trot up.
- How close to the trot up the horse needs riding.

This is a consideration with horses that don't trot up well. It is not advisable to start a three-day event knowing your horse is not 100 per cent sound so masking lameness at this stage should not be necessary however older horses may be a little stiff and move better after exercise or some horses may not move well and improve after exercise so may require riding closer to the trot up and preparation may have to be done around this. It doesn't look good to present a sweaty horse so ample time must be given after work for the horse to dry and be groomed so remember to take into account:

- How long it takes to get the horse ready.
- How long it takes to prepare the tack.
- How long it takes to get to the trot up.

Preparing the horse

The horse will need a thorough groom or bath and all the stable stains must be removed. I prefer to put a rug on the horse after bathing to prevent the horse getting dusty, especially if stabled on shavings. Likewise stable bandages are put on any white legs and feet are picked and scrubbed out. The mane and tail are washed and plaited and a hood put on the horse to prevent rubbing and to protect the mane if the horse rolls. A tail bandage is put on the tail and a final trim is given to whiskers, feathers, bridle path and tail.

Preparing the tack

The horse must be presented in a snaffle bridle with reins or a trot up chain. The bridle is given a thorough clean and the buckles and chain polished. Most horses look better presented in a cavesson noseband and the number must be attached to the bridle. Boots and bandages, although removed for the actual inspection must be cleaned and a smart rug selected that will keep the horse clean and warm. A schooling whip may also be needed if the horse is lazy in-hand.

Final touches:

These are to be done just before leaving the stable to go to the trot up:

- Remove rugs, stable bandages and hood
- Brush horse off and wipe over with a dry cloth
- Apply quarter markings (optional) and secure with hairspray
- Put on trot up rug, folding forward if the horse has quarter markings
- Brush out tail. Apply a small amount of baby oil to the bottom, brush through and reapply tail bandage
- Sponge eyes, nose and dock
- Apply fly spray if necessary
- Pick out feet.
- Put on boots or bandages
- Put on bridle and number
- Take horse out of stable, brush pasterns, clean insides of feet
- Oil feet inside and out.

The horse is now ready to go to the trot up, take with you the following in a bucket or bag:

- Body brush
- Tail brush/comb
- Hoof pick
- Damp sponge
- Dry towel
- Baby oil
- Hoof oil and brush
- Fly spray and cloth
- Scissors

The trot up

When arriving at the trot up find out how many horses there are before you. The horse should be kept walking at this stage. When there are ten horses before you remove boots and bandages. Remove the rug; the horse must not get cold so this may have to stay on until the last minute. Give the horse a final wipe over, remove the tail bandage and brush the tail, sponge the dock and check that the insides of the feet are still clean and apply more hoof oil, then keep the horse moving until the stewards call for you. If all goes well put the boots and rug back on to take back to the stable.

THE HOLDING BOX

If the ground jury do not think that a horse is sound they can either fail you straight away or refer the horse to the 'holding box'. Here the vet will examine the horse, discuss what they have found with the rider and advise what to do. The rider then has to make the decision on whether to re-present the horse or to withdraw from the competition. If he chooses to re-present the vet will discuss the problem with the ground jury and advise whether or not he thinks that the horse is fit to compete. The groom is permitted to go into the holding box and should take a rug in case there is a long wait.

AFTER THE TROT UP

If the horse is still fresh or doing dressage the next day he may require more work after the trot up. Once the horse is finished for the day remove plaits and make him comfortable. Hand grazing for twenty minutes will again relax the horse if he got a little tense after the trot up. Shortly after the trot up times will be given for the dressage, there are usually two days of dressage and it is luck of the draw as to which day you are on.

If your horse is early to go the next day then prepare as much as possible the night before. Thoroughly clean all tack and prepare a clean saddle cloth with the number sewn on and a clean set of boots/bandages for working in. The horse's stud holes will also need to be cleaned and plugged.

DRESSAGE DAYS

The next two days not only involve the dressage but also preparing for the cross-country day. It depends when you do your test as to which order you do things in so your schedule may differ from this outline.

Preparing for Dressage

Make a plan working back from the time of the test, for example:

11.45   Test

11.15   Rider gets on

11.10   Horse ready

11.00   Tack up

10.50   Stud up

10.30   Final touches (as for trot up)

09.45   Plait

09.00   Wash off/let horse relax

08.15   Ride

07.00   Feed

This is a simple plan and always be prepared for things to change, the horse may have been quite relaxed but may sense a change in atmosphere as the competition begins and therefore require more work before the test.

Try to allow the horse to have some time alone in between exercise and preparation. Make sure the horse is drinking plenty and note when he last staled before tacking up for the test as this could affect his performance.

Turn out for dressage

The horse should be turned out for the dressage as for the trot up.

Tack: Studs

Boots/bandages for warm up

Tail bandage

Saddle

Bridle

Number

The following equipment needs to go to the dressage:

Body brush

Tail brush

Sponge

Towel

Hoof pick

Scissors

Fly repellent and cloth

Hoof oil

Spare studs and kit

Rug

Drink for the rider

Copy of the test

Running order

While your horse is warming up ask the steward if they are on time and how many horses there are to go before your rider. The horse will have to have a tack check and this can be done before or after the test; some riders prefer after as the steward will feel inside the mouth to check the bit which upsets some horses.

When the horse before yours enters the arena make the final preparations to your horse. Remove boots/bandages, remove tail bandage, wipe over, apply more fly repellent if necessary, apply hoof oil. Some horses may not stand to allow all of this to be done and final preparations should be as brief as possible.

Make sure that the rider drops his whip before entering the arena.

AFTER THE TEST

Put the boots back on and take the horse back to the stable. Remove plaits etc and allow the horse to rest.

Preparations for cross-country day

If your horse does dressage on the first day preparations for the cross-country day can be done the day before, however if you are near the end then some preparations will need to be done earlier.

Practice jump

At some point the rider may want to jump the horse. This can only be done at certain times when a FEI steward is there to watch. Times for this are usually posted in the stable manager's office; plan with the rider a suitable time. Studs and boots including over-reach boots will need to be worn for this, along with the horse's cross-country tack.

Walk the cross-country course

It is a good idea for the groom to walk the course, if possible with the rider. Not only is it interesting to see what your horses and rider will be jumping but it gives you an idea of what direction they are heading and where each fence is and this is very helpful if they are unfortunate enough to have a problem and you need to go onto the course to them.

Aid points

The Speed and Endurance tests consists of four phases:

Phase A   Roads and tracks
Phase B   Steeplechase
Phase C   Roads and tracks
Phase D   Cross-country

This is where a good back-up team is essential and the groom must find out where everything is if all is to run smoothly on the day. It is important to go to the following places, find out how to get there, how long it takes and what facilities will be there.

Start of phase A
Start of phase B
Finish of phase B/Start of C
Aid point of phase C
'C box'
'D box'
Route from 'D box' back to the stables

TRANSPORT

The layout of every three-day event is different, some have everything quite close and it is possible to walk, others are much more spread out and a vehicle is needed. If you don't have transport then speak to the stable manager who will arrange it for you, do this the day before as everyone will be very busy on cross-country day and it may be too late to organize.

If using your own vehicle it may be necessary to display a suitable pass allowing you to use the designated routes. In order to prevent the general public driving around the event the organizers can be very strict and failure to display a pass could prove to be disasterous.

THE 'C BOX'

Most three-day events have a 'C box' although a CCI★ may only have an Aid point. Find out where the farrier will be, where the water is and if there will be ice available. It is usual that the horse will be in the 'C box' for five or ten minutes depending on the level of the event and the weather conditions. Plan where best to position yourselves in the box, consider where the water is and whether there will be any shade.

THE 'D BOX' OR '10 MINUTE BOX'

Here the horse will have a break for ten minutes; this can often be extended if there is a hold up on the course. Again plan where you want to position yourself and where the water and ice is. Find some shade; bearing in mind the time of day (and therefore the shade) may well be different on the day. Try to ensure you are not too close to where the horses are starting and finishing.

When the horse finishes the cross-country they will either come back into the 'D box' to be washed down or may go into a separate area to prevent the 'D box' getting too crowded.

Preparation of equipment
Make lists of equipment needed for each phase:

HORSE

BRIDLE This must be given a thorough clean and all stitching checked. Reins must be a suitable length with good grip and rein stops. The buckles should have tape wrapped around them to ensure they do not come undone. A bootlace also needs to be attached to the headpiece, this is then tied to the top plait so that the bridle does not come off the horse should horse and rider be unlucky enough to fall.

SADDLE Give the saddle a thorough clean and check the stitching on girth straps and breastplate rings. Stirrup leathers must also be in good condition, check the stitching and wear at the holes. Ensure they are at the correct length and that there are sufficient spare holes for the rider to adjust the length if required.

NUMNAH/SADDLE PADS These should be lightweight and with good quality straps to secure to the saddle.

GIRTH This must be in good condition and a suitable length. The horse may well have lost weight during the week.

BREASTPLATES Clean thoroughly and check condition.

MARTINGALE Needs a thorough clean and check. There must also be enough holes to adjust the length as the rider often wants to alter this for the steeplechase.

OVERGIRTH Check the condition and length, it is important not to have this on the tightest hole at the beginning of the speed and endurance phase as it often needs to be tightened after the steeplechase.

CHAMOIS LEATHER This is used if the saddle slips back a lot.

BOOTS Should be in good condition but never use boots for the first time at a three-day event. Over-reach boots should also be ready and tubigrip cut to size if using.

NUMBER This needs to be attached to the bridle, breastplate or sewn on to the saddle pad.

Equipment for the steeplechase and 'C box'

Headcollar and rope

Suitable rug – depends on weather

Buckets x 2

Sponges x 2

Sweat scraper

Spare reins, stirrup leather and iron

Spare shoes

Spare studs and stud kit

Towels x 3

Hole punch

Hoof pick

Tape

Scissors

Drinks for rider

Lunge line if horse difficult

Plaiting bands.

Equipment for 'D box'

All of the above plus:

Buckets x 4

Sponges x2

Sweat scraper x 2

Rugs – Cooler x 2 and waterproof

Spare or change of Bridle

                      Bits

                      Girth

                      Numnah

                      Overgirth

                      XC Boots

                      Over-reach boots.

Towels x 4

Ice boots

Ice if not available

Rider's equipment

Jacket

Gloves

Whip

Chair

Programme

It is also important to prepare equipment at the stable so that everything is at hand when the horse has finished.

Ice

Ice boots

Dry cooler

Stable bandages and gamgee

First Aid – cotton wool $\Big\}$ to clean minor wounds
        sterile bowl
        Arnica pills and cream to apply to any bruising.

Preparing the horse

HEALTH Before starting on the cross-country (XC) it is important to be sure the horse is fit and well. Hopefully by this stage he has settled into the competition environment.

DRINKING If the horse hasn't been drinking very much throughout the week discuss this with the vet, it may be necessary at higher levels or in hot weather to arrange for the vet to tube fluids and electrolytes in to the horse before setting out on phase A. This needs to be discussed and a time set the day before as the vet will be very busy on XC day.

SHOES Check the shoes thoroughly and re-plug the stud holes. It may be necessary to change the shoes for XC for example if a horse wears bar shoes these are not ideal in wet conditions as they tend to be pulled off. Therefore if weather conditions are wet they will need to be changed to open heels. Check that the spare shoes fit the horse and are a set. The farrier can often make a mistake and the 'C box' is not a good place to find out! The stud holes on the spare shoes need cleaning and tapping. The spare studs can also be screwed in.

CLIPPING If weather conditions have got very hot or humid it may be necessary to clip the horse. Doing so after the dressage is best as it may make the horse more tense. If the horse is difficult to do it is best left as it is not worth causing the horse undue stress at this point and sedation is not an option due to dope testing.

DOPE TESTING Be prepared at any point throughout the event to be dope tested. Horses are selected at random and it is usually carried out on dressage or show jumping days. You will be required to take the horse to the vet stables where they will take both urine and blood samples.

A list of illegal substances is in the British Eventing Rule Book and is usually given to you at the start of the event. Always make sure any supplements or products you use, such as fly repellents or electrolytes have an FEI approved label on them as it is very easy to get caught out. If you have any concerns about the health of your horse always consult the vet before giving any medication be it oral or topical.

Brief helpers

You will need a minimum of two other helpers on XC day. Discuss with the rider exactly what he wants you to do at each aid point. Each helper must be clear on their responsibilities as it will only run smoothly if everyone knows what they are doing.

Times

XC times will be posted the evening before, make a copy of the times for each helper and a copy for the '10 minute box'.

Plan

Make a plan for the following day as with the dressage working back from the time the horse starts phase A.

SPEED AND ENDURANCE DAY

Feeding

XC day can often be a very early start as the horse will need to be fed his concentrates five hours before starting phase A. The horses should also be fed hay/haylage. The quantity will depend on what time the horse starts and whether the horse tends to pick at the hay or eat it very quickly (see chapter 5). The hay will need to be taken away four hours before the start of Phase A.

Water

The horse must not have the water taken away at any point. If you have any concerns regarding the quantities of water your horse has drunk then consult the vet. If the horse is needing to be tubed this should be done two hours before the horse starts.

Routine

Your prime concern is to keep your horse as relaxed as possible before he starts. Often the horse will hear the XC commentary and the more experienced will know what lies ahead; this can often cause them to become stressed, especially if they don't go until much later in the day. All horses are individuals and some will benefit from a walk out or hand graze whilst others become more uptight with this. Do whatever suits your horse, if you don't start until later in the day a short walk every two hours will prevent the horse from coming out stiff.

Equipment

At some point before starting you may need to take some equipment to the 'D box'. The earlier this is done the more likely you are to get a good spot. Make sure you don't take any equipment that you will need in the meantime. Having found a suitable place leave the equipment in its box at this stage as it will be safer and won't get wet if it rains. Water buckets can be filled but in hot weather the water will become warm so leave it until later.

Official time

There will be an official event time which can either be got from the stable manager's office or the start of phase A. You must synchronize your own watch with this to ensure you are on time – remember seconds are penalties.

Preparing the horse

The horse will need to be ready about half an hour before the start of phase A. Some riders prefer their horses to be plaited and others prefer the mane free, this is personal preference. If the horse is being plaited do so early enough to let him have a break before tacking up. This gives him a chance to have a drink. Try to encourage the horse to pass urine before starting to get him ready as they will be out for two hours or more and most horses are reluctant to stale outside the stable. Skipping out or shaking up the bed often does the trick. The horse will need to be groomed and have a tail bandage on. When tacking up everything must be fitted with extra care and shouldn't be rushed so leave extra time to do this.

ORDER OF TACK UP

Over-reach boots – if pull on ones these are best done before the studs.

Studs – make sure they are tight. You will need a spare set of studs to match the ones you have used. In some cases the studs will have to be changed in the 'D box'.

Tubigrip – if using under boots.

XC boots – make sure the straps are even and firm.

Tape boots.

Breast plate.

Martingale.

Chamois leather if being used.

Numnahs and saddle pads.

Saddle – girth must not be close to the top as it may go up more in the 'D box'. Do not fasten the overgirth yet.

Bridle – attach to top plait.

Put a rug over the horse to keep him warm.

Phase A

Before leaving for phase A make sure you have with you all of your equipment for the steeplechase and 'C box'. Skip out the stable and fill up the water buckets; check everything is ready for the horse coming back.

The horse may be led or ridden to the start; this often depends on the temperament of the horse. Get there ten to fifteen minutes before starting to

give the horse a chance to stretch his legs and settle. If he is becoming more uptight then it is better to stay somewhere quiet until closer to your time.

    Once the rider has got on rugs can be removed, girths checked and the overgirth done up. Have one last check you have everything, see the horse off; then to phase B as fast as you can.

*A horse tacked up
ready to start
phase A*

Phase B

There is usually one minute from finishing phase A and starting phase B, the horse may come in early and once he has crossed the finish of A you can check him. Nothing should have gone wrong but have a quick look over tack and boots and check the girth. There aren't usually any major tack changes but the rider may like the reins on a gag bit altered, all should be done as quickly as possible. At the same time your helpers need to go to the 'C box' to prepare water buckets and equipment. As the horse starts the steeplechase you need to make your way to the finish, position yourself a little way from the finish where the horse will come past you. Different riders will do different things at the end of the steeplechase; some will pull up after the finish and walk to let their horse recover, this could result in the horse tying up and it is preferential to keep the horse moving and gradually bring him back to trot and walk.

As the horse passes you, check that he hasn't lost a shoe and there are no obvious signs of discomfort or broken equipment. The horse continues on phase C and you must make your way to the 'C box' to get prepared.

Phase C

The procedure on phase C will vary depending on the level of event and the weather conditions. Until recently there was no compulsory halt on phase C but there would be an aid point shortly after the finish of the steeplechase where horses would be checked over briefly by the support team to ensure tack and boots were secure and the horse hadn't lost a shoe. Water is available and a farrier on stand-by. As it is so close to the end of the chase it is not ideal to have the horse pull up while still blowing hard so checks here should be brief and if possible done while the horse is on the move. This system is often still used at one star level or two-day events.

The 'C box'

A 'C box' has now been introduced at most three-day events. This is to give the horses more recovery time after the steeplechase and a chance for the vets to monitor horses more closely during speed and endurance. The position of the box will vary from event to event but is usually between 1 and 3km on phase C. It is a compulsory box and horses will stop for five or ten minutes depending on the level of competition and the weather; obviously in hot and humid conditions the horses take much longer to cool and recover.

By the time horse and rider are approaching the 'C box' your equipment should be laid out and ready. Water buckets should be filled. If the horse has lost a shoe warn the farrier and have the shoe ready.

The support team will have been thoroughly briefed and ready to do their job. As the horse comes in check the time, you will also have a steward giving you time checks.

One helper should meet the horse and put on the headcollar if the horse doesn't like being held by the bridle. This person is responsible throughout the ten minutes for keeping the horse relaxed and for walking the horse.

The vet will check the horse's heart rate and possibly the temperature. Ask what the readings are as it is useful to know.

As this is happening run up the stirrups and take the horse to the equipment. Your second helper should now:

Loosen the girth (optional)

Loosen the noseband (optional)

Check shoes, studs and boots

Check all other tack

Offer the horse water and sponge out the mouth

If the horse has lost a shoe do the above and then take the horse to the farrier. As long as the shoe is the correct fit it won't take too long to put back on. Having got the shoe replaced wash and walk the horse until the water coming off the horse feels cooler.

The third person washes the horse. The extent to which the horse is washed down will depend on the weather conditions, the more a horse can be cooled in the 'C box' the better chance he has of recovering for the next two phases. In very hot conditions it may be necessary to have two people washing and it is essential to work as a team and not get in each other's way.

Water should be applied to all areas of the horse, if wearing a square saddle pad fold the corners under the saddle flaps and wash as much as you can. After washing scrape and walk. If the horse is blowing hard he must be walked and washed at the same time. In cooler conditions it is not necessary to wash as much, judge by the horse's condition when he comes into the box.

After five minutes the vet may want to check the horse again. At this point adjust the saddle if necessary and tighten the girth and noseband.

The holder will need a towel to dry the reins, saddle and stirrup treads. The rider will get on at two minutes to go, walk around, tighten the girth and then the overgirth will be done.

One of the most common injuries a horse suffers at a three-day event is tendon injury to the forelimbs. Research has shown that a tendon is less tensile when heated, imagine how hot the legs are under the XC boots at this stage, the horse still has up to an hour to go and the XC course still to complete. With the tendons already very hot it is no wonder so many horses suffer tendon injuries at three-day events. To try and prevent this we have recently started to remove the front boots after the steeplechase and the horse carries out phase C without boots. There is a slight risk that the horse may knock himself but much more of a chance that the legs will cool a little and the boots can then be reapplied in the 'D box'.

The 'D box'

Once the horse has set off on phase C quickly pack up and on to the 'D box' or '10 minute box'. This is a compulsory halt at all two- and three-day events.

Have all of your equipment set out as you did in the 'C box', I find it useful to lay out a waterproof sheet and spread everything that I need.

- Spare shoes
- Spare studs, tap and spanner
- Scissors
- Tape
- Hole punch
- Spare or change of tack
- Spare boots
- Towels
- Grease and gloves
- Rugs
- 4 Water buckets filled – with ice in hot weather
- Sponges and sweat scrapers
- Ice boots in iced water ready for the horse finishing
- Have a chair ready for the rider with drinks, spare gloves and whip

Find out if there are any hold-ups on the course and if things are running to time. Ask others how the course is riding and if any fences are causing problems as the rider will not have heard anything up to this point.

As the horse comes into the 'D box' the same procedure should be carried out as in the 'C box'. After the vets have checked the horse take him to your equipment. I have found that aggressive cooling in the 'C box' has had my horses coming into the 'D box' much cooler, however the atmosphere of the cross-country will have probably made them a little

Equipment neatly set out in the 'D box'

A farrier will be present in the 'D box' to replace lost shoes

257

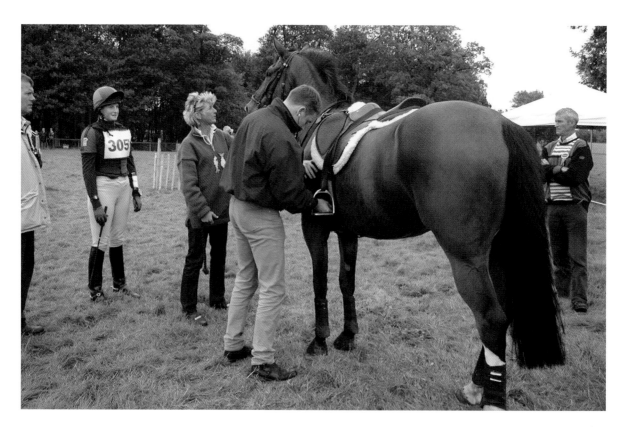

The vet will check the horse's heart rate when he comes into the 'D box'

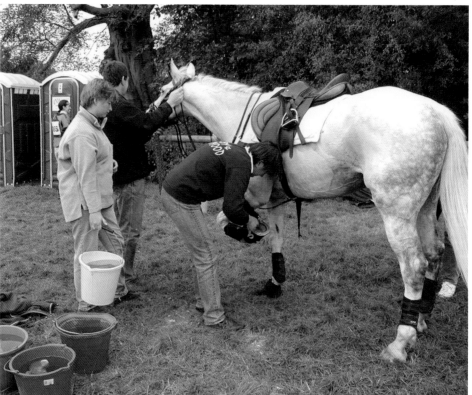

The studs must be checked in the 'D box'

stressed and it will be necessary to do some more cooling. Follow the same routine as in the 'C box' although there may be some small differences.

- Removing the saddle – some people choose to do this to cool the horse more effectively.
- Change of tack – the most common change of tack would be changing the bit; this is done quicker if the bit is already on a separate bridle.
- Change of studs – it is quite common to have to change the studs, the horse must be handled as quietly as possible and studs must be changed by a calm and efficient person as this can be a difficult job if the horse is uptight.
- Boots thoroughly checked and taped if necessary.
- If front boots were removed, check legs, towel dry, apply clean dry boots and tape.
- Continue washing until the horse is cool.
- Only apply rugs in very cool conditions as the horse will still be very hot and the cooler he starts the better.
- Keep the horse walking as much as possible.

The vet will check the horse again after five minutes. At five minutes replace or adjust the saddle and tighten the girths, towel dry reins, saddle and stirrup treads and apply the grease (optional).

At three minutes the rider gets on, tighten the girth, walk a circle and then do the overgirth. Once the rider is ready to go, follow him to the start box in case he has a problem getting the horse into the box.

At any point there may be a hold-up due to problems on the course. This could mean that you are in the box for much longer, possibly up to an hour in extreme cases. The horse must be kept as relaxed as possible, monitor his temperature and keep the horse walking. During a very long hold it may be necessary to stand for periods (in the shade if hot) and walk for periods. Your steward will keep you informed as to the situation and give you five minutes' notice as to when you will be started.

Preparation for horse finishing

When the horse sets off get your equipment ready for the horse finishing.

- Water buckets filled

- Ice boots ready
- Headcollar
- Rugs
- Stud equipment
- Ice – in a cool box
- Scissors
- Towels

Clear all other equipment away.

Some events will have a monitor in the 'ten minute box' so you will be able to watch the horse's progress; if not be sure to keep listening to the commentary while you are preparing for the finish.

If the horse has a fall and the rider or horse are unable to come back to the 'D box' then you will have to go to them, take with you a headcollar and rug.

Finish of cross-country

The vets will check your horse's temperature and pulse immediately after the horse has finished. You know your horse, notice how tired he looks, and compare this to how he finishes at one-day events.

Loosen girths and noseband, check for any obvious problems such as cuts or bumps.

The horse will not be released from the 'D box' until the vets are happy he has recovered well. Take the horse to your equipment and untack him. Use as much water as possible and wash all areas of the horse; scrape, walk and wash again. Continue this process until the water coming off the horse is cool. Whilst this is happening one helper can remove boots, check for cuts and apply ice to the legs. There are many different ice boots on the market but personally I prefer ice wrapped in a jay cloth and bandaged over as this stays much cooler. Ice should be removed after twenty minutes and applied every hour.

Remove the studs and offer the horse water in small quantities as he does not want to drink too much while still blowing. Monitor how the horse is recovering and how he is walking. Often horses do not pull up lame but lameness will show as the adrenalin comes down.

The vet will release the horse once he is happy with the temperature and pulse at which point the horse can be taken back to the stable.

On returning to the stables

By the time the horse has walked back to the stables he should have fully recovered but if not cooling and walking must continue. The stable should be prepared with plenty of bedding, two water buckets are advisable with electrolytes in one. Rug up according to temperature and how the horse is, I tend not to over rug at this stage as adrenalin is still up and the horse is likely to break out.

The horse needs to rest for a few hours but needs to be closely monitored, points to pay special attention to are:

- Drinking
- Droppings
- Urine
- How the horse is standing, does he look comfortable, is he resting any legs, digging at the bed, looking colicy?
- Eating – offer about 1.8kg (4lb) of hay/haylage to be fed from the ground.
- Legs – I continue to ice the front legs for twenty minutes every hour for two or three more sessions.
- Give a small concentrate feed two hours after finishing.

If the horse has recovered well and all the above is looking normal this is the routine I follow for the rest of the day.

Approximately three hours after finishing the cross-country remove ice and bandages from the legs and allow twenty minutes for any problems to show. Thoroughly check the legs for any heat or swelling that may have come up. Remove all rugs to trot the horse up on a hard surface, after higher level competition it is expected that there may be slight stiffness but not lameness. Check the legs again out of the stable.

If all looks well I tend to let the horse graze for about thirty minutes. If the horse has shown stiffness many people are tempted to walk him continuously until the stables close in the hope of preventing further stiffness, this to me is pointless at this stage as the horse has to stand in the stable overnight and will stiffen up again. Rest at this stage is much more valuable although hand grazing may mentally help relax them and help ones who have gone off their feed.

It is personal preference as to what you do with the legs overnight. I tend to apply stable bandages over cotton wraps, this helps prevent the legs from filling and will not irritate. Ice tight or clay is commonly used, this is applied to the legs and bandaged over and it helps to give legs a much 'tighter' appearance. I don't like to use it as there is a danger of masking a problem, often a leg will feel very good the next day when the ice tight comes off and slight heat and filling is not recognized. The horse is then showjumped and more damage is done. If the horse does tend to get filled legs then use ice tight only if in no doubt that there may be a problem.

The stables usually close at 11.00 or 12.00 on cross-country night: closely monitor the horse until then but also allow him to rest. At some point the horse will need to be fed again, this feed should be his normal ration containing his supplements, often they may be picky over the feed but if it is left in it is usually finished by morning. If the horse is very reluctant to eat check the mouth isn't sore which may be causing discomfort, if this is the case apply bonjella which will numb the area. I feed ad lib hay/haylage at this stage and again I prefer to feed off the floor. Final checks to the water should be done as late as possible as they will drink a lot overnight.

Thought must be put into rugging up, magnetic rugs are often used but do be aware that the horse will probably be warmer than usual and do not over rug. The horse should then be left to a good night's rest.

Dealing with problems

The horse may have sustained an injury and although often this is easily recognized, at other times it may be very slight or take longer to show making diagnosis more difficult, this is why knowing your horse and close monitoring are essential.

CUTS/GRAZES

Assess the injury and decide whether veterinary assistance is required; this would be the case if needing stitching or antibiotics. Trot the horse up to see whether the injury is causing lameness or discomfort. Small cuts should be thoroughly cleaned with warm water and a dressing applied if it is an area that may get dirty or bedding in it especially if the horse is on shavings. If in doubt about how clean the cut is it is advisable to apply a poultice. There may be bruising around the injury and icing the area will help reduce inflammation and pain. More serious injuries will require the vet to check and deal with, they will also advise if it is wise for the horse to continue the competition.

MOST COMMON INJURIES

Over reach

Speedy cuts

Grazed stifles/knees

Boot rubs

Cut mouth

FOOT PROBLEMS

Many horses are prone to foot problems and these are the most common cause of lameness. The horse may have lost a shoe on the cross-country or bruised the sole if the ground is hard or rough in places on the roads and tracks. To diagnose the foot check for more heat in one foot and a strong digital pulse. Some horses will benefit from having a lost shoe replaced as soon as possible whilst others will benefit more from having the foot iced and possibly poulticed overnight then re-shod the following morning.

There are two ways of icing the foot.

1. Tubing – stand the horse in rubber buckets with iced water or crushed ice for twenty minutes every hour.
2. Packing the foot with crushed ice – crush the ice and pack into the sole of the foot, cover with a plastic bag and bandage to secure, leave for twenty minutes and repeat every hour.

If the horse is prone to corns or abscesses it is advisable to have the event farrier investigate the foot and advise whether to re-shoe immediately or treat the foot and put the shoe on next morning.

LEG PROBLEMS

COMMON INJURIES

- Jarred joints

- Tendon/ligament injury
- Twisted joint
- Bruising caused by hitting a fence

Diagnose the lame leg and site of injury. Quite often the horse will not be lame immediately after finishing the cross-country as the adrenalin is running quite high, cases where the horse does pull up lame usually indicate a foot problem or more serious problems such as tying up or tendon problems. The vet will deal with this immediately. When lameness shows later it is important that an experienced person examines the horse and decides if the problem is one that can be dealt with and will not affect the horse long term or if it is more serious and show jumping the next day will be detrimental.

If it is decided that it is a more serious injury and the horse will not continue the competition then seek the vet's advice on how best to make the horse more comfortable for the night and travelling home.

Minor injuries are best dealt with by reducing inflammation as this then reduces pain. Use ice boots or cool boots for twenty minutes every hour, or for higher injuries hold ice wrapped in a cloth to the area. Continue for as long as possible until the stables close. The legs should be stable bandaged overnight to reduce swelling. Other treatments that will help reduce inflammation are cold hosing, whirlpool boots and massage.

BACK PROBLEMS/SORE MUSCLES

The horse may not be lame but suffering from a sore back or general stiffness through his muscles. At most three-day events a physiotherapist is available to treat your horse. A form must be filled in and handed into the stable manager's office to allow the treatment to take place. The physio will then assess the horse and treat accordingly; this usually involves the use of heat, magnetic, laser or massage to make the horse more comfortable.

ARNICA

Arnica is useful to relieve bruising and is not a banned substance. I tend to feed arnica tablets as a matter of course from the start of the event and often continue for a few days after.

Tack and equipment

At some point in-between treating and monitoring your horse you will need to sort out all the cross-country tack and equipment, clean and prepare for the next day.

- Make sure all equipment is collected from the 'D box'.
- Put dirty boots, saddle cloths, girths etc into a bag to be taken home for washing. (Leather boots should be cleaned with the tack.)
- All tack must be thoroughly cleaned and checked for damage.
- Prepare bridle for trot up.
- Prepare tack and equipment for show jumping.

SHOW JUMPING DAY

The horse must be presented to the ground jury for a second inspection to allow them to continue to the show jump phase. This is the exact same format as the first trot up.

Preparation for final vets' inspection

The stables usually open at 5.30am; the trot up can be as early as 8.00am but is usually 9.00am. It is advisable to start as early as possible as often the horse will not be feeling as good as the night before due to stiffness. This is the procedure I follow:

- Arrive at the stables at opening time.
- General check over how the horse looks, state of bed, droppings, any leftover feed, how much water he has drunk – this will give an indication to how he has been overnight.
- Feed concentrates.
- Remove bandages.
- Skip out.
- Fill water buckets.
- Remove rugs, take horse out and trot up – if there is stiffness or lameness you have plenty of time to deal with it.
- It is usual the horse will be ridden or have a good hand walk before the

trot up to loosen him up, I find it more beneficial to do this closer to the trot up.

- Plait.
- Groom/apply tail bandage.
- If the horse has a minor injury it may be necessary to have an assistant to be dealing with this while you are plaiting.
- The physio may also need to treat again.
- The horse will need riding for about twenty minutes; this should be timed to have the horse back at the stable half an hour before he leaves for the trot up to give you time to do the finishing touches.
- Leave for the trot up half an hour before your time, the horse should be kept warm and walking.
- If the horse is very stiff it is often more beneficial to ride to the trot up as it is easier to keep them at a good walk and also gets the adrenalin up.
- If there is still soreness in a leg keep the ice boots on until the last minute.
- Trot the horse a few times to make sure he looks all right, this saves the embarrassment of presenting a lame horse, the ground jury may be lenient towards a stiff horse but will not except lameness.
- Once presented the same procedure takes place as the first trot up.

Show jumping

The show jumping usually takes place in two stages, the lower placed horses jumping in the morning and the top half in the afternoon. If your horse is jumping in the morning you will need to get ready straight away, if he is jumping later in the day then he should be left to rest. Make sure he has hay and water, and if he is likely to roll put in a rug and hood.

A running order will be released shortly after the trot up giving each horse's time to show jump. Again make a plan working back allowing time to prepare the horse and warm up for jumping.

Parade

At some point all the horses remaining in the competition will be required to do a mounted parade. This takes place in the main arena usually before the top half start to jump, or after the last horse has jumped before the prize giving. The horse should be turned out smartly; the atmosphere often gets them very excited, good leg protection is necessary to prevent injury.

The horse should be turned out as smartly for the show jump as he was for the dressage and the same procedure can be followed.

EQUIPMENT TO TAKE TO SHOW JUMPING

- Headcollar and rope
- Brush
- Sponge
- Hoof pick
- Spare studs and kit
- Scissors
- Towel
- Rug
- Fly spray
- Hoof oil
- Bottle of water

The rider may ride the horse to the show jumping or may want to watch and you may have to lead the horse there. It may be necessary to stand or walk the horse in a quiet area if he has got uptight by the parade until the rider gets on. You may need an assistant to change boots or equipment.

A plan should have been made as to when the rider will want to get on, have a running order with you so you know exactly where they are up to. Once the rider is on you may be required to assist in the collecting ring with the practice fence, this needs to run very smoothly so is an advantage to have an extra person to help.

If possible before the horse goes into the ring :
- Pick out feet
- Check studs and boots
- Check girth

AFTER SHOW JUMPING

Depending on when your horse jumped the horse may then go back to the stables or wait around for prize giving. If it is the latter loosen the girth, put a rug over the horse and wait in a quiet place.

Prize giving

Before going into the ring for prize giving give a quick brush off and apply hoof oil. Again it may be necessary to put on suitable leg protection if the horse is likely to get excited. It may be necessary to go into the ring to hold your horse if your rider is receiving a prize, make sure you are well turned out!

GROOM'S PRIZE

Most three-day events present a prize to the groom who they feel has taken best care of their horse and turned out to the highest standard.

Care after show jumping

* Un-tack
* Remove studs
* Wash down
* Un-plait
* Rug up accordingly

If you are travelling home that day it is advisable to allow the horse a few hours to recover, especially if you have a long journey. Leave the horse to relax with food and water while you pack the horsebox. It is highly likely at this stage the horse will be dehydrated and if you have a long journey ahead it may be necessary to have the vet put fluids into him as he will be unlikely to drink much while travelling home.

Passports must be collected from the stable manager's office along with dressage sheets. Stables must be mucked out and left as you found them.

Prepare the horse to travel, bandages can be applied but caution must be taken not to get them too tight as the legs may fill whilst travelling. On long journeys I prefer to use leg wraps.

During the journey home the horse must be checked on a regular basis as they may still be stressed from the competition causing them to break out and rugs may need changing. (See chapter 8.)

Care of the horse post competition is discussed in the next chapter.

CHAPTER 12

Roughing Off

'Roughing off' is the term given to the period of time in which it takes to adjust a horse that is competition or hunting fit to being 'let down' and prepared to be turned out in the field for a holiday. It is common practice for hunters to be turned away during the spring and summer and event horses during the winter. It is often not done with dressage and showjumpers as it is possible to compete all year round. In my experience I have found advantages and disadvantages to giving horses long periods of rest.

ADVANTAGES

- Physically the horse's legs and body have time to recover from a period of hard training. This can be a disadvantage if the horse has an injury that is then not being managed correctly.
- Psychologically some horses need to 'switch off' and have a break.
- Labour saving.
- Saves money.

DISADVANTAGES

- Psychologically some horses don't adapt to being turned out. This may lead to injury and weight loss.

- The horse will become fat and unfit. More work then has to be put into the horse to reduce weight and to condition muscles. This in turn means more wear and tear on the limbs which leads to injury and lameness.

- In the case of event horses I find the winter months an ideal time to work on dressage or showjumping problems, or to train the horse to the next level at which he will be competing the following season. I tend to give my horses a short break at the end of the season and they unwind mentally but don't lose a great deal of fitness. A horse that is less fit and more relaxed is much easier to train.

Before roughing off your horses, consider the advantages and disadvantages. Every horse should be treated as an individual and have his own programme.

TIME PERIOD

Many people don't bother with the roughing off period and turn the horses away the day after the last competition or day's hunting. There is often a risk of injury if this is done. I have often heard people say that their horse finished a three-day event perfectly sound. He was turned out the following day and came in twelve weeks later with a tendon injury. This is rarely the case. What actually happens is the horse has sustained a slight injury during competition, which often goes unnoticed. When turned out he then gallops around causing further damage. This is not seen as the horse's legs are not being closely monitored and hence there is a fairly serious injury, which could have been avoided.

The roughing off period will take between one to two weeks, depending on the following factors.

Level of fitness

The more fit a horse is the longer he should be given to 'let down'. One that has been competing at novice/intermediate eventing, dressage, showjumping or lightly hunted should take about a week. An advanced three-day event horse or fully fit hunter should be monitored for longer and will take up to two weeks.

Temperament

Every horse has his own personality. Some are more independent and like nothing else than to be put in the field and given a break from us. Others however don't adapt as well to the drastic change in routine. They will often be at the field gate after a few hours begging to be brought in. Don't choose to ignore this as the horse is then likely to injure himself by galloping around or even jumping out of the field. An unhappy horse is also prone to losing condition.

Health and soundness

The general health and soundness of the horse must be considered. Sufficient time must be allowed to monitor your horse before turning him away fully. Horses that are in hard training are more predisposed to injury or soundness problems and should be monitored for longer. If the horse has returned from a major competition special attention should be paid to the legs. I have experienced cases when a tendon injury has not shown for a few days after it was sustained. When a horse is in work the legs often appear much tighter. When the work is reduced they will often fill more. If bandages are worn in the stable they should be removed for the period to avoid masking a problem. During the rest period the regular worming programme should continue and vaccinations kept up to date.

Condition

This will vary depending on the time of year. In the spring and summer when the weather is warm and the grass is plentiful, it is advantageous to turn out a horse that is lacking condition. This is not the case in winter when the cold weather and lack of nutrition will not help the cause. Each horse will need feeding differently. In spring it may be necessary to restrict the grazing to prevent the horse becoming too fat as this does not help when the time comes to get the horse fit again. During the winter months it will often be necessary to continue feeding the horse even when he is turned away.

PROCEDURE

Work

Psychologically some horses do not adapt from being in hard work to doing nothing at all. Consequently when turned out they tend to gallop around and are at risk of injury. During the first week of roughing off the horse should be hacked in walk for an hour cutting back to half an hour by the end of the week. If you have a horse walker, half an hour slow walking would also benefit. During the second week hack for half an hour every other day and half an hour on the walker.

Feeding

A hunter being turned out in the spring should get all his nutritional requirements from the grass. Care should be taken at the beginning not to feed too much as it could lead to colic or laminitis. During the winter months most horses will require feeding in the field. It is not likely he will require the same diet as he did when in work. First consider the condition of the horse. Does he need to gain weight because he is too light at the end of the season or does he need to maintain his current weight? Gradually change the diet over the period of a week. The concentrate ration should be reduced and the roughage increased. If the horse needs to gain condition feed slow release energy such as fibre and oil. High starch diets are more likely to cause freshness.

Grooming

Thorough grooming should be stopped to allow the build up of natural oils in the coat. This will help protect from the wet and cold. The horse should still be checked over every day paying particular attention to the legs. The feet should also be picked out.

Rugs

During the week the number of rugs the horse is wearing should be reduced. In winter this will encourage the growth of winter coat. It may be necessary for the more thoroughbred type horse to be turned out in a New Zealand rug. Also horses in poor condition must be kept warm otherwise fat supplies will be used for warmth and further condition will be lost.

Shoeing

Your horses' feet require the same amount of attention as when in work. Continue on your regular shoeing programme. I find my horses last a week longer during the winter months as horn growth is slower. It is advisable when turning out in company to remove the hind shoes. Even the most well-mannered horse can get excited and kick by mistake. Discuss the front feet with your farrier. He may advise that the feet would benefit from a period without shoes. Some feet are not strong enough to cope, especially in wet conditions. Whatever the choice it is important the horse comes from his holiday with feet in good, healthy condition to start work on the roads. During the period in the field regular checks should be made for lost shoes and risen clenches.

Turn out period

Most horses will be accustomed to a daily turn out period. During the roughing off period increase the length of time the horse is out for. Initially your horse may expect to come in after his usual time period and will often become unsettled. If this becomes a problem the following may help:

1. Turn out after exercise.
2. Turn out when hungry and he will want to eat rather than play around.
3. Make sure your horse is warm enough. In winter it may be necessary to wear a rug.
4. If you are turning a number of horses out together it is often best to start them in pairs. Give each pair a few days to settle together before they are turned out as a group.
5. Avoid turning out odd numbers together as one horse usually gets left out and can cause distress which could lead to injury or loss of condition.
6. As the horse mentally starts to switch off he is less likely to want to come in. If the horse becomes unsettled at the prospect of being left out at night give a feed in the evening as most likely he is wanting to come in to be fed.

HOW LONG TO GIVE YOUR HORSE OFF

Consider the following when deciding how long to give your horse off.

Health and soundness

This is one of the most important factors to consider. If your horse ended the season with a specific injury it is important to follow your vet's advice. Horses with low grade lameness due to joint conditions often don't benefit from long periods of rest as they become stiffer. The less fit a horse becomes the more work will have to be put in to get him fit again. This is added wear and tear on the joints.

Level of fitness

The level of fitness the horse is at the end of the season and the level required for the next season has some significance in the amount of time you give him off. For example a horse competing at novice level does not require the same degree of fitness as a horse aiming for Badminton. A horse that has been very fit in the past will be much easier to condition than one that has not been properly fit before.

Age

It is not until a horse reaches the age of six or seven that physically he is fully mature. A horse develops muscle through a combination of good nutrition and correct training and work. In my opinion the young horse does not benefit from long periods of rest in the field. Condition is often lost very quickly and muscle has to be built up again. Short periods of rest allow for a mental break and give time to recover from growing pains. The older horse often does not do well turned away. During the winter months condition is often lost and the horse will come in looking poor. Older horses are often stiff and are better kept in light work such as horse walking combined with turn out.

Condition/weight

Some horses will gain weight very quickly when not working, especially during the spring and summer months. This is not an advantage when getting the horse fit again. A fat horse will need more work which is added stress to the legs. Avoid allowing horses with leg injuries or soundness problems to get fat. Other horses lose condition very quickly when not working. Both muscle tone and weight can be lost and again more work has to be done to regain these. Every horse is different and you will only discover what suits your horse when you have had them for a few years. Some will change with age for example one horse I have as a youngster dropped weight and muscle tone drastically when he had a holiday. As he has aged and become much stronger he maintains his condition well.

Future plans

It is important to plan for the coming season to decide how long a holiday to give. Your fittening programme should work back from your first competition date. I advise that you allow a week or two spare as there is likely to be some setback along the way.

Epilogue

The secret of success in equestrian sport is not only down to good horses and riders: care and preparation of the horse both at home and during competition plays a very important role.

In writing this book I hope that I have shown the importance of good stable management and the difference it can make to performance. My aim has been to be as practical as possible, sharing with you the knowledge and experiences that I have gained over the years. In recent years I have worked mainly with three-day event horses but the information which I have acquired is appropriate for anyone caring for horses. I hope this will be a useful guide to a wide range of people from grooms to exam students and for all horse owners wishing to compete, in any discipline at any level, and who want to care for their horses in a professional manner.

Index

appetite 2
Azoturia 107-9

bandages 164-70
    exercise 164-70
    polo wraps 165
    stable 165-6
    travel 166
    surgical 166
    knee and hock 166
    tail 167, 185
    travel 186
bandaging 169-70
bathing 33-4
behaviour 2
bits 140-2
    snaffle 131, 141
    three ring gag 141-2
    American gag 141-2
    (for) double bridle 142
boot injuries 163-4
boots 156-64
    brushing 156-7, 158, 161
    over-reach 157, 158, 159, 161, 187
    speedy cut 157, 160, 161
    choice of, 157
    work 158
    competition boots 158-63

tendon 160
    fitting guidelines 162-3
    poultice 167
    knee 187
breastplates 138-40
    hunting 139
    Aintree 139
    cleaning 153-4
bridles 130-2
    competition 131-2
    cleaning 152-3

clippers, care of 64-5
clipping 55-65
    when to 55-6
    types 56-7
    preparation 57-8
    procedure 58-63
    records 65
colic 105-7
competition, care of horse at 203-10
    before departure 215
    on arrival 215-18
    afterwards 230-3
competition, preparation 203-10
    pre-season 203-4
    leading up to event 205-10
    day before 210

condition monitoring 91-9
condition scoring 93-5
cross-country 222-8
    preparation 222-5, 244-5
    round 225
    afterwards 225-8
    walking course 245

dehydration 80-4
dressage at competitions 218-20
    preparation 218-19
    at the arena 219-20
    after test 220
dressage at three-day events 242-50
    preparation 243
    after test 244
    turn out 243-4
    preparation of equipment 246-9
    preparing horse 249-50
dressage training (for fitness) 121-2

electrolytes 84-6

fat horses 102
feeding 66-110
    basic rules 66-9
    choices of diet 69-72
    fibre 73
    protein 73, 75
    starch 74
    oil 74-5
    vitamins 76
    traditional 76
    compound 76
    roughage 77-9
    supplements 86-91
    difficult feeders 99-100
    at a competition 236-7
feet 19-25
    care of 19-25
    balance 19-20
    problems 21-22
first aid kit 16-18
fittening 111-29
    aims 112-13
    planning programme 113-14
    types of work 115-21

    checks to make 126-8
foregirth 140

girth sleeve 148
girths 146-9
    synthetic 146-7
    leather 147-8
    Balding 147
    Atherstone 147
    three fold 147
    webbing 148
    manmade 148
grooming and turnout 26-54
    kit 27-9
    methods 29-36
    heavy coats 34-5
    machines 35
    sick horses 35
    grass-kept horses 35
    tired horses 35

hay 77-9
haylage 78-9
horse health 1-18
    daily checks 3
    see also illness and injury
horseboxes 175-83
    maintenance 175-6
    fittings 176-80
    preparing for travel 181-3
    see also trailers, travelling
hot clothing 33

illness and injury 128
    COPD 109-10
    stress 189-90
    dehydration 80, 190
    weight loss 191
    cuts, grazes 262-3
    foot problems 263
    leg problems 263-4
    back problems 264

jump training (for fitness) 122-4

laying manes 44-5
laying tails 45

loading 192-7
    preparations 192
    procedure 192-3
    difficult loaders 193-5
    unloading 195-7
lungeing/long reining 124-5

martingales 136-7
    running 136-7
    standing 137-8
    cleaning 153-4

nosebands 132-35
    cavesson 132
    flash 133
    drop 133-4
    Grakle 134-5
numbers 237
numnahs 150-1
    dressage 150
    show jumping 150-1
    cross-country 151
    hunting 151

overgirths 149-50

plaiting 28-9
pulling manes 36-9, 45-9
pulling tails 39-40, 49-51
pulse 6

quartering 32-3, 52-3

records, maintaining 15-16
reins 135-6
    dressage 135
    show jumping 136
    cross-country 136
    hunting 136
respiration 6
ropes 184
roughing off 269-75
    advantages 269
    disadvantages 269-70
    time period 270-1
    procedure 272-5
rugs 184-8

sweat 184-5
cooler 185
summer sheet 185
day 185
at competitions 238

saddle pads 151
saddlery, care of 151-5
saddles 142-5
    fitting 143-6
    cleaning 154
shoes/shoeing 19-25, 273
show jumping, at competitions 220-2
    preparation 220-1
    collecting ring 221
    afterwards 221-2
show jumping day at 3-day events 265-8
    vets' inspection 265-6
    show jumping 266
    parade 266
    equipment 267
    afterwards 267-8
    prize giving 268
    care afterwards 268
speed and endurance day at 3-day event
    250-65
    feeding 250-1
    equipment 251
    Phase A 252-3
    Phase B 253-4
    Phase C 254-8
    'C box' 254-6
    'D box' 256-5
    finish 260-2
stables 3
stabling at competitions 228-30, 236
stirrup irons 146
stirrup leathers 146
stud guard 149
stud holes 23-4
    care of 173
studs 23-4, 170-4
    advantages 170
    disadvantages 171
    types 171-2
    fitting 173
    care of 174

surcingles 185
    elastic 185
    rollers 185
    cross 185
swimming 125

tack and equipment 130-74
    competition rules 142
    for competitions 205-10
teeth, care of 9-11
temperature 6
three-day events, care of horses at 234-68
    departure 235
    arrival 235-9
    equipment 246-8
    see also dressage
trailers 180-1
travel by sea 199
travelling 175-202
    bad travellers 183
    preparations 183-9
    overseas 188-9
    care during 197-8

trimming 28-9, 41-4
    tails 41
    feathers 41-2
    coronet band 43
    whiskers 43
    under the jaw 43
trot up day at 3-day event 239-42
    planning 239-40
    preparing horse 240
    preparing tack 240
    final touches 240
    in holding box 242
    afterwards 242
turnout for competitions 52-4

vaccinations 13-14

water 79-86
weight 95-7
    using a weigh tape 95
    using a weighbridge 96-7
    loss 101-2